THE BRECON BEACONS
NATIONAL PARK

THE BRECON BEACONS
NATIONAL PARK

Roger Thomas

Webb & Bower

MICHAEL JOSEPH

Acknowledgements

All the photographs were taken by Colin Horsman, for the
Countryside Commission.

First published in Great Britain 1987 by
Webb & Bower (Publishers) Limited
9 Colleton Crescent, Exeter, Devon EX2 4BY
in association with Michael Joseph Limited
27 Wright's Lane, London W8 5SL
and The Countryside Commission,
John Dower House, Crescent Place,
Cheltenham, Glos GL50 3RA

Designed by Ron Pickless

Production by Nick Facer/Rob Kendrew

Illustrations by Rosamund Gendle/Ralph Stobart

Text and new photographs Copyright © The Countryside Commission
Illustrations Copyright © Webb & Bower (Publishers) Ltd

British Library Cataloguing in Publication Data
The National parks of Britain.
Brecon Beacons
1. National parks and reserves — England —
Guide-books 2. England — Description and
travel — 1971- — Guide-books.
I. Thomas, Roger, *1947*–
914.2'04858 SB484.G7.

ISBN 0–86350–136–2

Typeset in Great Britain by Keyspools Ltd., Golborne, Lancs.

Printed and bound in Hong Kong by Mandarin Offset.

Contents

Preface

The Brecon Beacons is one of ten national parks which were established in the 1950s. These largely upland and coastal areas represent the finest landscapes in England and Wales and present us all with opportunities to savour breathtaking scenery, to take part in invigorating outdoor activites, to experience rural community life, and most importantly, to relax in peaceful surroundings.

The designation of national parks is the product of those who had the vision, more than fifty years ago, to see that ways were found to ensure that the best of our countryside should be recognized and protected, that the way of life therein should be sustained, and that public access for open-air recreation should be encouraged.

As the government planned Britain's post-war reconstruction, John Dower, architect, rambler and national park enthusiast, was asked to report on how the national park ideal adopted in other countries could work for England and Wales. An important consideration was the ownership of land within the parks. Unlike other countries where large tracts of land are in public ownership, and thus national parks can be owned by the nation, here in Britain most of the land within the national parks was, and still is, privately owned. John Dower's report was published in 1945 and its recommendations accepted. Two years later another report drafted by a committee chaired by Sir Arthur Hobhouse proposed an administrative system for the parks, and this was embodied in the National Parks and Access to the Countryside Act 1949.

This Act set up the National Parks Commission to designate national parks and advise on their administration. In 1968 the National Parks Commission became the Countryside Commission but we continue to have national responsibility for our national parks which are administered by local government, either through committees of the county councils or independent planning boards.

This guide to the landscape, settlements and natural history of the Brecon Beacons National Park is one of a series on all ten parks. As well as helping the visitor appreciate the park and its attractions, the guides outline the achievements of and pressures facing the national park authorities today.

Our national parks are a vital asset, and we all have a duty to care for and conserve them. Learning about the parks and their value to us all is a crucial step in creating more awareness of the importance of the national parks so that each of us can play our part in seeing that they are protected for all to enjoy.

Sir Derek Barber
Chairman
Countryside Commission

Introduction

Introductions are deceptively difficult things to write. They establish a tone, set a scene and (hopefully) whet an appetite. In the case of the Brecon Beacons, there is one additional problem. How do you encapsulate, within a few hundred words, an area of over 500 square miles?

The task is made no easier by the fact that I have been fortunate enough to regard the Beacons as my own special backyard for most of my life. My home is right on the park boundary. My first tentative forays, unaccompanied by parents, into the world outside led me, inevitably, into these hills and mountains. Over the years, the Beacons have become, for me, a familiar backyard – but one that I never take for granted; and one that is difficult to explain away in the confines of this introduction.

So does this area have an overriding personality

View from the top. Looking south-east towards the upper Neuadd reservoir from Pen y Fan, the highest point in south Wales.

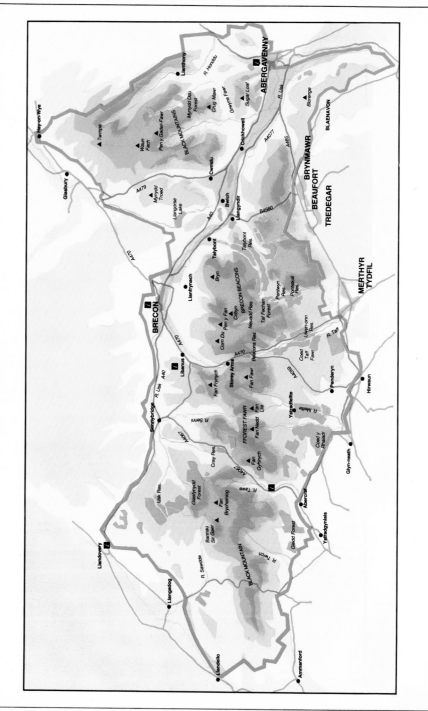

which can be pinned down swiftly and succinctly? Well, yes and no. On face value, I could simply say that here we have the highest mountains in south Wales – and leave it more or less at that. But I also feel compelled to describe the park's waterfalls, wooded gorges, caves, green lowlands and gentle river valleys, none of which conforms to the standard highland image.

I am also acutely aware of the confusing complexities of the park. Mountains are, of course, the dominant feature here: over half of the park's 519 square miles is over 1,000 feet high, much of this upland rising consistently to altitudes of over 2,000 feet. But these mountains confound straightforward definitions. The Brecon Beacons themselves rise to the distinctive table-topped summit of Pen y Fan, at 2,907 ft (886 m) the highest peak in south Wales. Yet these mountains represent only one-quarter of an undulating highland range, contained within the park, which rolls westwards from the Wales/England border for over forty miles almost to the doorstep of Swansea.

The Brecon Beacons, then, although the geographical centre and etymological springboard of the park, by no means define its extent. Here begins even more confusion. It is by no means unknown for first-time visitors to this area to end up in completely the wrong place. The reason? They mix up two of the park's other upland ranges – the Black Mountains (plural) along the eastern border with the Black Mountain (singular) in the far west. A fourth mountain block, known as Fforest Fawr (sandwiched between the Brecon Beacons and Black Mountain) completes the quartet of upland ranges in the park. The map may speak louder than words to those still confused by it all.

These mountains, the 'backbone' of the park, are formed from Old Red Sandstones and divide the ancient rocks of mid-Wales from the south Wales coalfield. They relinquish their hold to the south, where outcropping bands of Carboniferous Limestone and Millstone Grit create a different landscape of wooded gorges, waterfalls and caves. River and lakeland scenery are also important components within the park's landscape. The chief river here is the Usk, which cuts across the mountain chain – sometimes in a most attractive, broad vale – as it flows south-eastwards. Many of south Wales's main rivers rise in the park, while the north-east is drained by the Wye and the west by the Tywi.

In the final analysis, the mountains are the main

Facing
The Brecon Beacons
National Park.

magnet. Their promise of scenic grandeur and wide, open spaces – fulfilled by the large stretches of open and common land over which there is a long tradition of free access – draws visitors from far and wide. Many have to make only a short journey. The park's proximity – and long-term vulnerability – to the highly populated south-east of Wales, in which the vast majority of the Principality's two and three-quarter million inhabitants are concentrated, played a major part in its creation, in April 1957 (the last of Britain's ten national parks to be thus designated).

This particular national park's southern boundary – surely the most predictable and emphatic of them all – coincides with the abrupt transition from rural to industrial south Wales. On other points of the compass, too, the boundaries are in parts fairly self-evident. The park shares its borderline with Wales and England along stretches in the east. To the north, sections of the Usk valley and the Mynydd Epynt military range help define the boundary, whilst in the west the park ends along the verdant Vale of Tywi. Administratively, the park covers a lot of ground. Sixty-six per cent of its area lies in the county of Powys, seventeen per cent in Dyfed,

Not a wilderness into which to venture unprepared. Fan Foel (on the left) and the ridge of Bannau Sir Gaer in the formidable Black Mountain.

eleven per cent in Gwent and six per cent in Mid Glamorgan.

Another problem with introductions is knowing when to stop; so I will conclude with the hope that the contents of this book will add to your knowledge and enjoyment of this green and sturdy mass of mountains which embraces some of Britain's finest and most exhilarating expanses of open countryside. But do not take my word for it; let the Beacons themselves have the final say.

Author's note: In order to avoid any confusion over the precise meaning of the term 'Brecon Beacons' I have adopted the following usage throughout the text. When I use the terms 'Beacons' or 'Brecon Beacons', they refer to the entire park. Only when these are preceded by the word 'central' do they refer to the specific mountain range from which the park takes its name.

1 The making of the Beacons

In the last century, the Rev H Elvet Lewis of Llanelli spent an evening in Brecon. It must have been a memorable one, for he described the view looking southwards to Pen y Fan in the following glowing terms: '. . . and when a clear evening draws out the near heights in outline, leaving on the triple summit a thin haze of blue, or of faint gold at sunset, one may in a single glimpse catch the difference between the softer charm of Southern landscapes and the more rugged grandeur of the North'. His golden sunset might have been a little faint, but more than a faint tinge of purple colours his prose. This is understandable, for eighteenth- and nineteenth-century romantics, unencumbered by the weighty empiricism of the sciences, had made respectable a florid, overblown writing style. William Wordsworth, doyen of the romantic poets and suspected harbinger of the dreaded purple prose, has a lot to answer for.

One can look upon it in another way. Those earlier writers were in many ways privileged. Free from the heavy baggage of reference books and diligent research, they were able to embark upon imaginative flights of fancy – occasionally with surprisingly prescient, illuminative results. Our good reverend, for example, would probably have possessed scant knowledge, if any, of the geological structure of those peaks above Brecon. He nevertheless managed to pinpoint, in a sentence, the 'softer charm' of the Brecon Beacons as opposed to that of rugged Snowdonia in the north.

If this seems like a roundabout way in which to begin a chapter dedicated to the geology of the Brecon Beacons National Park, please accept the following observations in mitigation. That 'softer charm' is the consequence of a particular geological structure. The relationship between geology and scenery is a direct and fascinating one. An understanding – even basic knowledge – of the former can enhance by leaps and bounds our appreciation and enjoyment of the latter. But there are pitfalls. No geological exposition, however

Geological section illustrating north-south rock strata.

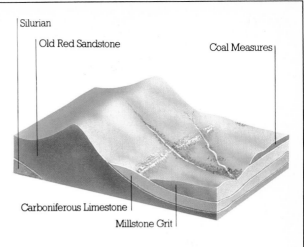

Silurian

Old Red Sandstone

Coal Measures

Carboniferous Limestone

Millstone Grit

thorough, should detract from our capacity to experience that subjective, intuitive response evoked by high mountains, windswept moorlands and pastoral river valleys. For my part, I will attempt to steer clear of the two evils of purple prose at the one extreme, and academic arrogance at the other.

Having declared my interests – and possibly prejudices – I shall begin. As it happens, the Rev Lewis got it about right. His lyrical observations merely confirm detailed comparative research into underlying rock structures. The Brecon Beacons pitted against the mountains of north Wales are, in geological terms, somewhat uncomplicated. There is nothing soft or straightforward about Snowdonia, a lucky dip of sedimentary and volcanic rocks in which it is difficult to unravel the jumble of geological complexities. The Beacons, on the other hand, are reassuringly homogeneous. For a start, they consist of sedimentary rocks only, a structure deriving from materials laid down in beds mainly by rivers and seas. And within that broad categorization, one type of rock from the Devonian period – Old Red Sandstone – tends to dominate.

The overall geological pattern, then, is characterized by its uniformity. In topographical terms, this translates itself into a conspicuous consistency of landscape, apart from one major exception where the southern 'dip' slope, rising in an easy gradient, suddenly plunges down a steep, north-facing escarpment (see the geological diagram). Overall, though, the Brecon Beacons is a park of few surprises. Unlike Snowdonia, this is a mountainous area of rounded, smooth outlines, gradual gradients, unbroken horizons, big skies and deceptively gentle profiles.

The Beacons are highlands pure and simple – and highlands at their most subtle. With a few exceptions, there are no great accelerations or reversals of scale here apart from that severe northern scarp face. Consistent height – much of it over 2,000 feet – and gradual inclines disguise the true altitude of its summits. Although they rise to nearly 3,000 feet (the highest land in south Wales), these peaks appear to be less lofty than they really are. Make no mistake though: this is deceptive – dangerously deceptive – terrain; the Beacons ranges are mountains in every sense of the word. Visually, the vistas are harmonious, the views extending far and wide across undulations unbroken by intrusive elements. The Beacons, to me, have always resembled the petrified waves, dipped in green, of a huge inland sea.

The simple geological explanation which accounts for this consistency is given by the single rock type that steals the limelight in the Beacons. Old Red Sandstone forms the bedrock of the park, covering around two-thirds of its land area. The Beacons are founded on this sandstone rock; and Pen y Fan, the distinctive sandstone summit, represents the park's geological and geographical centre.

Old Red Sandstone is a sedimentary rock, laid down in the Devonian period 395–345 million years ago. It is a generic term for rocks formed from gravels, sands and muds (respectively, the conglomerates, sandstones and marls) deposited those many million years ago by rivers flowing

Horizontal bands of Brownstones can be seen to good effect in this north-facing escarpment between Pen y Fan and, in the distance, Cribyn.

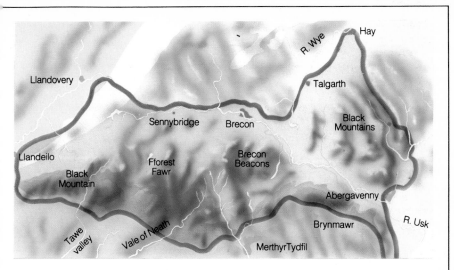

The geology of the park; an overview.

- ◣ National park boundary
- Ordovician
- Carboniferous Limestone
- Millstone Grit
- Coal Measures
- Silurian
- Old Red Sandstone

down from mountains and across coastal plains in the area now occupied by the Beacons. Some rock surfaces to this day display ripple marks like those of sandy river beds.

There are at least five subdivisions of the Old Red Sandstone that covers most of the park, each one having implications for scenery and landscape. But before we can delve into the geological detail, we initially need to stand back a little and take a wide overview, firstly of the main geological ingredients in the park landscape, and secondly of the external forces which have moulded and modified them.

These two major considerations can be broadly identified as the characteristics of the park's various underlying rocks; and the subsequent action on them of the elemental forces of water, weather and ice. In this respect, the Beacons can be regarded as a most compliant and co-operative teacher – a geological text book, no less – for the relationship between theory and practice is a very strong one here. As anyone who has studied the subject will tell you, the Beacons provide definitive example after example of classic geomorphological landforms, photographs of which bring much welcome visual relief to pages of text and theory.

Firstly, let us look at the overall geological pattern of the park. Old Red Sandstones of the Devonian period may dominate, but they are not the oldest rocks here. For the complete picture, we have to go back even further, not quite to the age of the Cambrian and truly ancient pre-Cambrian rocks found in other parts of Wales, but nevertheless to a time pre-dating the Devonian period. Our starting point in the Beacons is marked by the Ordovician and Silurian rocks, 500–395 million years old, that accumulated gradually in the shallowing seas which once covered this area. These rocks were formed from the thick layers of mud and sand that settled under the seas and subsequently consolidated. They underlie most of west Wales, and make an appearance in the extreme north-western margin of the park in a line roughly parallel to the road between Llandovery and Llandeilo.

Rocks younger than those of the Devonian period also appear in the park. These are from the Carboniferous period, 345–280 million years ago, when the terrestrial conditions of Devonian times were replaced by seas and estuaries. These Carboniferous rocks, cropping out in a narrow band along the southern boundary of the park, represent the only major incursion into a landscape otherwise carved from rocks of Devonian age.

In terms of a chronological hierarchy we have, then, in the Beacons, four major geological periods – the Ordovician, Silurian, Devonian and Carboniferous – embracing a time span from 500 to approaching 280 million years ago. To begin at the beginning, the Ordovician rocks are here represented by mudstones and grits formed in the beds of that great sea that once covered parts of central and western Wales. The Silurian shales and sandstones with marine shelly fossils also come from this thick sea bed. These are the tough, hard rocks which can be seen around Llandovery and Llandeilo, underlying the slopes of the Tywi valley and rising to well over 1,000 feet on the Trichrug ridge a few miles due east of Llandeilo.

The transitional phase between Silurian and Devonian is represented by Tilestones and the lowest Red Marls, both of which are found in valleys and the lower hills. The former are so-called because of the ease with which they split into thin slabs, ideal for roofing materials. They lie in a narrow band, next to the Silurian outcrop in the west of the park. Specifically, they can be seen in the Sawdde valley (which runs from the foothills of the Black Mountain to join the River Tywi at Llangadog) and in a quarry approximately one mile east of Halfway, a hamlet on the A40 Llandovery to Brecon road. The Red Marls in places contain marine fossils. These rocks take us right into the next major geological phase, for the marls which lie exposed

The tufty moors of Fforest Fawr decline abruptly into the more cultivated farmlands of the Senni valley.

along the fertile Vale of Usk, and which also form the foothills of the Black Mountains, are a subdivision of the Old Red Sandstones of the Devonian period. Next up from the marls are the Senni Beds, thus named because of their exposure along the Senni and other rivers flowing northwards into the Usk from the Beacons and Fforest Fawr uplands. These sandstones, green or dull red in colour, in some places are solid and substantial, in others broken and flaky, resulting in an unpredictable terrain over which rivers and streams make irregular progress as they tumble downwards into the Usk valley.

The Senni Beds were succeeded by the most significant Old Red Sandstone subdivision of all: the famous Brownstones from which are formed the park's main mountain ranges. From Bannau Sir Gaer (sometimes referred to as the Carmarthen Fans) in the Black Mountain, across Fforest Fawr and the Beacons proper to the borderland Black Mountains, much of the high ground comprises Brownstones, hard rocks that have weathered into smooth hills, many over 2,000 feet in height. These resistant rocks, layer after layer of them, form a band around 1,200 to 1,400 feet thick consisting of interbedded

Red Marls, brown sandstones and conglomerates.
   Their strata, apparently horizontal in many
places, can be seen exposed in the north-facing
escarpments that sweep across the park. Below the
2,460 ft (750 m) Bannau Sir Gaer in the Black
Mountain, for example, the Brownstones lie in layers
above the scree slopes. Brownstones are nowhere
better exposed to view than in the steep northern
face of Pen y Fan. The escarpment here consists of a
regular 'staircase' pattern of rocks, the harder
bands standing out as steps and shelves. Pen y Fan
is kind enough to lead us into our penultimate
subdivision of Old Red Sandstones. The peak is
quite clearly capped with another rock, even
harder than the Brownstones. This is a very resistant
blend of conglomerates and sandstones known as
Plateau Beds, a rock which accounts for the flattish
'table top' summits of the Beacons. The two highest
peaks, Pen y Fan at 2,907 ft (886 m) and neighbouring
Corn Du at 2,863 ft (873 m) achieve their altitude
through the protective umbrella provided by
isolated fragments of these tough Plateau Beds. At
Bannau Sir Gaer, the topmost fifty feet or so consists
of Plateau Beds lying with a visible discordance on

Llyn Cwm Llwch, a textbook example of a glacial lake, beneath the pronounced north-facing scarp in the central Beacons.

the Brownstones. This is where the Middle Old Red Sandstone is entirely missing in Wales, leaving the Upper to rest directly on the Lower. Other high ground that has attained summit status, thanks to a capping of Plateau Beds above the general level of surrounding upland, includes Waun Fach (2,660 ft – 810 m) and Pen y Gadair-Fawr (2,624 ft – 800 m) in the Black Mountains south-east of Talgarth.

Yet another version of this distinctive layering, and the varying levels of resistance it implies, is identified cartographically by the word *tarren* or *darren* on the 1:50,000 Series Ordnance Survey map (for example, Darren Lwyd above the Gospel Pass south of Hay-on-Wye). These are rugged cliffs, high above some of the valleys enclosed within the Black Mountains, the result of steps produced by extra hard layers of Brownstones.

In the Beacons the youngest beds of Old Red Sandstone are the Grey Grits, a mixture of quartz grits and sandstones. These crop out in the south of the park next to the rocks of the succeeding Carboniferous period. The lonely Bryniau Gleision uplands (the 'Blue-Grey Hills') between the Taf Fechan and Talybont reservoirs are formed from them, as is some of the high ground between Taf Fawr and the village of Penderyn.

Gradually, the Grey Grits, together with their Devonian predecessors, disappear beneath the succeeding rocks of the Carboniferous period, which began 345 million years ago and lasted for the next sixty-five million years. These 'newcomers' dominate the surface along the southern edge of the park, heralding a profound change not limited simply to geology and topography. It is difficult to exaggerate the importance of this southern outcrop. We will deal with its distinctive geology shortly; but before we do, its wider relevance begs attention.

The southern boundary of the park, which largely coincides with this outcrop, is no random accident. Its line has been determined not by the underlying rocks *per se*, but by man's exploitation of them. In this context, it is not too melodramatic to say that the geology of this area can be expressed, in socio-economic terms, as the confluence of rural and industrial Wales. The key to it all is coal – more precisely, Coal Measures, the youngest of the Carboniferous rocks in the Beacons, though they only make fleeting appearances within the park itself in small areas near Ystradgynlais and Coelbren and eastwards of Brynmawr in the Clydach gorge. As the youngest, uppermost of the

Carboniferous rocks, they lie above limestones and grits, also of the Carboniferous period.

There is, I believe, no more emphatic a border to any of our national parks than the 'great divide' determined by these Coal Measures. If this sounds a trifle partisan, it is perhaps understandable, for I happen to live right on this boundary. At the village of Cefn-coed-y-cymmer, a mile or so north of the former iron- and steel-producing town of Merthyr Tydfil, the road climbs a gentle slope. Around and about, the catalytic ingredients of coal, iron ore and limestone coincided, triggering off an eighteenth-century industrial explosion that changed the face of south Wales: the south Wales, that is, of the coal-bearing valleys, which suffered large-scale devastation as hundreds of mines were sunk and thousands of workers and their families poured into the new, tightly packed terraced communities that grew up along the valley sides.

The hills to the north of the Coal Measures remained more or less unaffected, their unspoilt, rural persona strangely heightened by such close proximity to a teeming, scarred landscape. If nothing else, the industrial consequences of these Coal Measures have given the Brecon Beacons

Henrhyd Falls, on the southern edge of the national park where rural meets industrial.

National Park a clear-cut, self-evident franchise. The dramatic, definitive contrasts at either side of that sudden 'great divide' contain within them all the arguments in favour of protection and conservation. If you still need convincing, follow the A470 northwards as it crests the rise just above my home in Cefn Coed. At this point, quite unexpectedly, Wales discards its urban coat – there is no gradual

High ground in the Black Mountain commands sweeping views northwards across the Vale of Tywi to the distant hills of mid-Wales.

transition zone – as the towering limestone cliffs above the village come into view along with a flaming beacon on the roadside sign marking the entrance to the park. The experience is more or less the same along the entire southern boundary, at towns such as Ammanford, Ystradgynlais, Glynneath, Hirwaun, Brynmawr, Blaenavon and Pontypool.

This diversion in our geological narrative has hopefully cast the story in a slightly different light. Geology is not, ultimately, sterile theory; neither is it only manifest in geomorphological features, particular forms of landscape and the like. It can also have profound consequences in social, industrial, economic – and human – terms.

So within the park, there is little evidence of Coal Measures. The two older Carboniferous rocks – Carboniferous Limestone and Millstone Grit – are the main components of the outcropping band, which varies in width between around two and seven miles, along the park's southern boundary. The rocks were formed when the terrestrial conditions that prevailed in the land-based Devonian period were replaced by shallow seas. The materials that accumulated – including corals, shellfish and other sea-creatures such as brachiopods and crinoids (sea-lilies) – formed the limestones, the oldest of the Carboniferous rocks. Such was the abundance of this sea-based 'raw material' that the rock here sometimes consists almost entirely of their skeletal remains, often fragmentary but sometimes quite unbroken.

Overlying this rock is Millstone Grit (once used for millstones in the north of England, hence its name). In the Beacons, this rock consists, in its lower layers, of Basal Grit (massive white quartz conglomerates and sandstones). Then come the Middle Shales (grey or blue shales and mudstones, sometimes with insubstantial beds of coal that were never mined) followed, in its upper layers, by the so-called Farewell Rock (massive beds of sandstone

The limestone country around Ystradfellte displays all the classic features associated with this type of rock.

lying below the next Carboniferous series, the Coal Measures, so that when miners struck them they knew they had bidden 'farewell' to their coal seams).

The variable nature of these grits suggests that they were accumulated in or near the estuaries of large rivers. Correspondingly, they offer bands of varying resistance to erosion which have striking scenic consequences in the Beacons. In fact, both Carboniferous Limestone and Millstone Grit show characteristic patterns of erosion which produce the distinctive landscape, quite unlike anything else in the park, which exists in concentrated areas along its southern boundary.

Limestone rock is fissured and permeable, with two basic properties: it is soluble in rain and river water, and extensively transversed by joints.

Rivers, as soon as they leave the unyielding sandstones, slice through the limestones, forming steep-sided gorges and serrated, shady ravines, sometimes disappearing completely into swallow holes and cave systems. And when they reach the Millstone Grits, their courses carve out yet more changes. Rivers plunge over their harder upper beds, eroding the softer shales beneath to form rapids and waterfalls (the creation of which has also been influenced by faulting in the rock).

The Carboniferous rocks bring to the park a welcome variation in landscape. Old Red Sandstone does not have its own way entirely. Bare-flanked, agoraphobic hillsides with their wide, open spaces occasionally subside into narrow valleys, claustrophobic caverns and wooded gorges. This complex alternative landform is at its best just south of the hamlet of Ystradfellte, where the belt of Carboniferous Limestone and Millstone Grit is at its broadest.

I first discovered this compelling, memorable corner of the park in the early Sixties. It must have left a deep impression on me, for I can still recall, quite clearly, the precise occasion of the visit. As a schoolboy with an enforced interest in geography, I had duly tramped to the summit of Pen y Fan, taken part in a school expedition to the boggy wastes of the Carmarthen Fans and followed the remote Grwyne Fawr trackway in the Black Mountains. The Beacons Park, I had concluded, was an area of lumpy mountains. Then I discovered Ystradfellte.

I had heard vague stories about caves, inaccessible waterfalls and the like so, together with a few colleagues, set off south from Ystradfellte on one wet October day intent on following the course of the River Mellte. Armed with only a soggy Ordnance Survey map (there were no guide-books or well-established footpaths in those days), our tentative steps soon led us to a particularly chilly, gloomy bend in the river. Suddenly, there was no more river. It had been swallowed up by the gargantuan, gaping mouth of Porth yr Ogof.

Today, well-equipped parties of potholers are a common sight at this remarkable cave entrance, probably the largest in Wales, before they disappear along with the Mellte into the darkness. We backtracked up and across the top of the cave to rejoin the river as it emerged, a quarter of a mile or so downstream, in a deep pool. This disappearing trick is characteristic of the rivers in this area. Fissures and pot-holes in the easily soluble

Porth yr Ogof's awesome portal, gateway for many a group of pot-holers intent on subterranean exploration of Ystradfellte's limestone country.

limestone swallow up complete watercourses (especially in the drier summer months), leaving pebbly river beds entirely dry. You do not have to be a wet-suited speleologist to catch sight and sound of these gurgling underground waterways. Some, visible through fissures, flow quite near the surface. At the approach to Porth yr Ogof, for example, small breaks in the hillside reveal subterranean water channels into which parts of the Mellte have already disappeared.

A further mile on our journey downstream from Porth yr Ogof took us into the heart of 'Waterfall Country'. We did not know it then, but we had, in geological terms, crossed from limestone to the overlying sandstones of the Millstone Grit series, their junction occurring about three-quarters of a mile south of the cave. The Mellte, as soon as it meets the Millstone Grits, begins its tumble down a flight of spectacular waterfalls. First, we came across Sgwd Clun-gwyn ('White Meadow Fall'), followed by Sgwd Isaf Clun-gwyn ('Lower White Meadow Fall'), likened by some to a 'miniature Niagara', then a third, smaller cascade, Sgwd y Pannwr ('Fall of the Fuller'). The middle fall, Sgwd Isaf Clun-gwyn, is typical of the way in which differential erosion is at work here, the waterfall developing at a point where a fault crossing the river brought hard Millstone Grit sandstones upstream into contact with softer shales of the same series downstream.

We had been looking for a fourth waterfall, Sgwd yr Eira ('Fall of Snow'), apparently the most spectacular of all. Our failure to find it was not surprising – an experience shared by many. We made the common mistake of confusing its location, for it is sited not on the Mellte, but on the Hepste, a tributary a little way to the east.

Sgwd yr Eira is the most famous of all the falls, not, one suspects, for its size, but for the novelty value provided by the path that leads right behind its drop of water, allowing walkers an inside look at a waterfall without getting wet. This dry 'walk behind the falls' is possible thanks to the washing away of a five foot wide band of soft, black shales beneath a twenty foot thick upper ledge of tough sandstone.

My initiation into 'Waterfall Country' was a baptism in more than one sense of the word. I could not have become any wetter as we trudged southwards on that rainy October day, having to wade the swollen Mellte at one point before

Ystradfellte's 'Waterfall Country'.

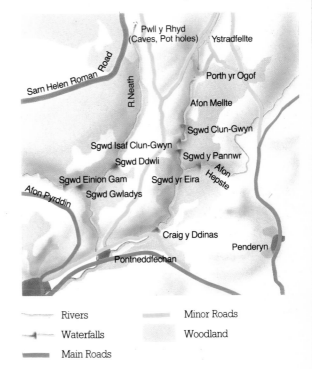

emerging back in civilization at Pontneddfechan near Glyn-neath. My appetite, though, was firmly whetted. I have since been back countless times; possibly too many as far as this book is concerned, for I am inclined to the opinion that this part of the park itself merits an entire tome – never mind the part of one chapter.

In these pages, I will have to content myself with a personal selection of not-to-be-missed sites. They

Sgwd Clun-gwyn, the
northernmost of the
series of classic waterfalls
on the River Mellte.

include, of course, the aforementioned falls together
with those of Sgwd Gwladys, Sgwd Einion Gam and
Henrhyd. The first two are on the Pyrddin, a
tributary of the Neath, accessible by path from
Pontneddfechan. The route is initially a well-
founded – and extremely attractive – one as it
follows the banks of the swift-flowing Neath to its
junction with the Pyrddin. From here, it is a short
walk to Sgwd Gwladys, a waterfall that closely
resembles Sgwd yr Eira in its pronounced,
overhanging upper ledge. Sgwd Einion Gam,
further upstream, is much more difficult to
approach. The path becomes increasingly
indistinct, suddenly petering out at the base of great
cliffs in a mossy, almost primeval, bend in the river.
From here, it is a case of wading and scrambling to
this eighty foot (twenty-five metre) waterfall which
some reckon to be the best of all. It is, unarguably,
the most remote. As one writer has rightly
commented: '. . . most of the beauties [of Waterfall
Country] lie out of the direct route, and require
some search'.

   The Henrhyd Falls, a little further west near the
village of Coelbren, are the most easily accessible
of the lot. A National Trust property, these falls (the

singular should apply really, for there is only the one proper waterfall here) on the Nant Lech take a shuddering, unbroken ninety foot plunge into a precipitous, wooded chasm just inside the park boundary. Interestingly, a thin seam of coal outcrops in the cliff face around the falls. Visitors in need of more conclusive proof of its existence need only return to the car park and gaze southwards across the fields to the vast, lunar-like landscape of open-cast mineworkings that fill the skyline. Industrial south Wales, as I have already pointed out, does not start with a whimper.

Waterfalls are by no means the only ingredients in this variform Carboniferous outcrop. The rocks here display a veritable cornucopia of features and curious formations both above and below ground. Limestone's highly soluble nature as it is eroded in fissures and joints causes swallow and shake holes to appear, ultimately creating a vast, labyrinthine underworld of cave systems and passageways. Porth yr Ogof may be the most conspicuous cave entrance of all, but the caverns that attract the lion's share of attention, understandably, are those at Dan-yr-Ogof near Abercraf in the upper Tawe valley. These are well-organized showcaves where the public are taken on guided tours through the first part of an extensive cave system, discovered early this century, which contains spectacular calcite (limestone-based) stalagmite and stalactite formations. An enormous 'Cathedral Cavern', over 150 feet long and with a drop of around seventy feet from ceiling to floor, is also open to the public.

Across the valley from Dan-yr-Ogof, at Ogof Ffynnon-ddu, there is a major underground complex which surveys have confirmed as the deepest and one of the longest in Britain. Agen Allwedd, in another pronounced limestone area near Llangattock, is also a particularly long cave with over twelve miles of passageways. Of the countless swallow holes in the park, none is more dramatic than the deep fissure known as Cwm Pwll y Rhyd. It is located on the upper reaches of the River Neath a few hundred yards south of Pont Pwll y Rhyd, at the entrance to the so-called – though optimistically named – 'Grand Canyon' gorge. In dry weather, there is usually no sign of any water at this point: it has long since disappeared into smaller swallow holes and fissures upstream. After rain, the river is usually in full spate, only to pour its contents over a shelf into the deep, gaping basin of Cwm Pwll y Rhyd before re-emerging a short distance

After a dry spell, little or no water spills into this gaping limestone swallow hole, Cwm Pwll y Rhyd, for the river has already disappeared underground. But when the River Neath is in full spate, the story is different.

downstream at the White Lady Cave.

A rash of shake holes covers the plateaux of Mynydd Llangynidr and Mynydd Llangattock, as aerial photographs of this area reveal. Looking not unlike the aftermath of a bombing raid, these holes pit the surface in exceptional numbers (there are, in fact, more shake holes here than anywhere else in Britain). They are caused, in the main, by the collapse of overlying Millstone Grit into the caves which riddle the limestone below.

Carboniferous Limestone and Millstone Grit also produce classic features along the skyline. The former sometimes outcrop as 'scars', sharp, jagged cliffs above steep escarpments. The Craig y Cilau Nature Reserve, west of Llangattock, the Taf Fawr valley just north of Merthyr Tydfil, and the hills above the Craig-y-nos Country Park near Dan-yr-Ogof are just three of the many craggy limestone 'scars' in the southern belt of the park. The Millstone Grit above the limestone also rises into high ground in the form of north-facing escarpments, such as those fringing Gwaun Cefnygarreg in the hills east of Ystradfellte. Along the southern slopes of the Black Mountains due north of Crickhowell, there is a 2,302 ft (701 m) peak – Pen Cerrig-calch – unique in the park. This is the only limestone summit in a mountainous area otherwise dominated by sandstones. Its name gives it away, for *calch* is Welsh for lime. Pen Cerrig-calch is an isolated last remnant of Carboniferous Limestone (capped with Millstone Grit) which was once linked to the main outcrop further south.

The park's topography and landscape features are, therefore, the sum total of many influences. The underlying rock succession, important though it is, is by no means the only determining factor at work. We have seen, for example, the dramatic effects which rainfall and rivers have on the limestones in the Carboniferous outcrop. Many other forces and agents have also made their mark, disrupting and modifying the basic fabric of the Beacons.

Earth movements on a slow, inexorable and massive scale have played a disruptive, distorting role. The main backbone of the park – that great line of Old Red Sandstone mountains that stretch from the Carmarthen Fans to the Wales/England border – was raised high and tilted slightly southwards by such shifts in the earth's crust. The southerly band of Carboniferous rocks displays more evidence of this disturbance. Faults, fractures, uplifts and folds all occur here, breaking up outcrops (and even, as we

have seen in the case of Sgwd Isaf Clun-gwyn,
influencing the development of waterfalls). A
number of major fault zones run across the south of
the park, most notably the fault that travels east-
north-eastwards from Pontneddfechan, a
continuation of the Vale of Neath Disturbance (a line
now followed by the eponymous river). The Craig y
Ddinas and Bwa Maen rocks at Pontneddfechan are
memorable manifestations of this great weakness.
Both rocks are located a short distance east of the
village. Craig y Ddinas thrusts itself out of the
ground to a height of about 150 feet, its exposed
limestone face lined with tilting bands of strata. Little
wonder, then, that this is a popular rock-climbing
venue. Bwa Maen is, geologically speaking, even
more interesting. Its Welsh name ('Bow of Stone')
reflects the way in which the rock has been
squeezed from a horizontal to near vertical position
by earth movements, a process clearly identified by
arch-like folds in the rock strata.

The other major influence which has left a deep
impression on the Beacons is glaciation. Even
though the Ice Age started around two million years
ago, it is a very recent event if time is measured on a
geological clock. Few can claim ignorance of its
consequences in the Beacons, where its effects are
everywhere to be seen. We do not, for example,
have to search for obscure clues of its passage when
we gaze upwards to the summits of Pen y Fan and
Corn Du from the lanes east of Libanus. Directly
below the peaks lies Cwm Llwch, a shady,
semicircular hollow sculpted out almost into its final
shape by a glacier. There would have been a valley
here in pre-glacial times, subsequently enlarged as
the ice – which may have accumulated here in its
greatest depth – bit into the slopes and probably
scooped out a basin at the bottom of the cliffs. This
was subsequently occupied by the glacial lake of
Llyn Cwm Llwch when the valley was dammed by
deposition of material by the retreating glacier (as
described below).

The ice sheets were formed from snow that easily
settled on the high, mountainous terrain in the
Beacons. From these heights, they ground their way
downwards as glaciers, wearing away at the
landscape and changing valley profiles from the 'V'-
shaped configuration to a wider, rounded 'U'-shape.
The snow that accumulated in hollows at the heads
of glaciers led to the creation of the huge
semicircular, amphitheatre-like hollows known as
cwms or cirques, similar to Cwm Llwch, that are

Dark stone and inky-
black waters at Llyn y Fan
Fawr, the remote Black
Mountain lake.

The twin peaks of Pen y Fan and Corn Du in the central Beacons.

such a feature of the north-facing scarps in the park. Just west of Cwm Llwch, for example, is Craig Cerrig-gleisiad (now a national nature reserve). The dramatic, atmospheric hollow below these cliffs was formed in a similar way, though its characteristic steep sides and back were possibly carved by snow rather than ice.

Glaciers also had a profound effect on landscapes to the south, polishing and planing the surfaces of Basal Grit exposed to their passage. Interestingly, evidence of the direction in which the glaciers travelled is etched into stone in the form of striations, parallel 'scratch marks' made in the rocks by angular boulders embedded in the passing ice sheets. These are particularly common in the Millstone Grit surfaces around Ystradfellte, and also in the area east of the Tawe valley.

As the glaciers pushed and scraped their way downslope, they had a 'snowplough' effect, collecting piles of material at their fronts as well as in and on the main body of the ice sheet. When the ice gradually melted, this material – a mixture of boulders, gravel and glacial debris – was left to form mounds or moraines. These moraines can have a marked effect on the landscape. Waters collected behind some, creating lakes such as Llyn Cwm Llwch, and the remote, myth-laden twins of Llyn y Fan Fach and Llyn y Fan Fawr in the Black Mountain. Llangorse Lake (Llyn Syfaddan), at over one mile in length the largest natural lake in south Wales, partially owes its existence to a moraine of bouldery gravel and clay. This barrier, deposited by the melting ice in the area between Llanfihangel Tal-y-Llyn and Talgarth, helped increase the depth

of the waters that collected in a rock basin scooped
out by a glacier.

The moraine just south of Llanfihangel Crucorney
was large enough to divert the courses of two
rivers, the Honddu and Monnow. They now take a
sharp, unnatural-looking swerve to the north-east in
the face of this barrier across their original direction
of flow southwards to Abergavenny. Similar
moraines, albeit not quite so large, are a common
sight in many parts of the park – look out for the
group of mounds clearly visible from the A470 at the
head of the Tarell valley near Storey Arms.

Materials picked up by the moving ice and
deposited when the glaciers melted are collectively
known as glacial 'drift'. In addition to moraines, this
drift also accounts for the deposits of clays which
were spread widely and more evenly across valley
floors and sides and the lower dipslopes,
concealing older rocks beneath and masking the
pre-existing landforms.

The termination of the Ice Age, around 10,000 to
12,000 years ago, almost marks the end of our story
of the forces that have shaped the Brecon Beacons
National Park. The period immediately following
this was characterized by prolonged freeze-thaw
conditions, when clayey drift tended to slide slowly
down the valley slopes over permanently frozen
subsoil and bedrock. Forming lobes and terraces, it
still covers large areas, now cut into by the upper
reaches of rivers, which in turn have carried fine-
grained soil downstream and spread it to produce
fertile valley land. Peaty acidic soils have formed on
the poorly drained, flattish summits and their gentle
southern slopes, a consequence of heavy rainfall
(around 100 inches a year) and the decaying of
matter from the plants which have grown on the
higher ground over the past 5,000 years.

The story of the making of the Beacons is a
continuing one, of course, as the forces of nature
imperceptibly but relentlessly go on wearing away
and re-shaping the landscape, day by day and hour
by hour.

2 From prehistoric to medieval times

History first began to clothe itself in substance and acquire real meaning for me when I stumbled across the ruins of Carreg Cennen Castle one bleak, November Sunday afternoon in the 1960s. This truly spectacular fortress – surely more authentically evocative of medieval times than our cosmeticized 'showpiece' castles such as Warwick and Caernarfon – attracts far less attention than it deserves, possibly due to its obscure location in the far west of the Brecon Beacons National Park.

Twenty years ago, visitors made their way to Carreg Cennen in numbers even slighter than today's still small figures. No one was around on that late autumn afternoon as I trudged through the muddy farmyard at the castle's base before climbing to the summit of the great limestone crag on which the gnarled defences are perched, like

The stumpy ruins of Carreg Cennen Castle bear witness to the ravages of weather and the struggles of man.

some precarious, oversized eagle's nest. Until that encounter, history had been, exclusively, an academic matter; interesting enough as a schoolboy subject though lacking the resonances that can give it extra depth and dimension.

The tumbledown, weatherbeaten walls of this atmospheric medieval pile, wet and cold to the touch, spoke in chilling tones of a brutal, harsh side to history. Never again would the subject simply be about lists of dates, matter-of-fact catalogues enlivened by the occasional heroic deed or romantic episode. Since then, I have been caught up in the ambivalent tug of history – should we admire man's doggedness and achievements or be appalled by our past? – at many ancient sites throughout the country. But most of all, because, I suppose, they lie on my doorstep, the Brecon Beacons have been my most articulate teacher.

The history of this part of south Wales leaves no stone unturned. Prehistoric man left his mark here, as did the Romans, Wales's Christian saints, native princes and Norman conquerors. In this chapter, we will confine ourselves to a 6,500-year time span which begins at Neolithic (New Stone Age) and ends in late medieval times. The park is an excellent timekeeper, for it provides us with everything we need – ancient burial chambers and standing stones, Iron Age hill camps, Roman roads and fortifications, early Christian sites, bare-boned medieval castles and comfortable manor houses – to chart our progress.

As measured by surviving sites, history in the Beacons commences during Neolithic times in around 3000 BC. Prior to that – going back to 10000 BC and the post-glacial period near the end of Palaeolithic (Old Stone Age) times – the park would probably have been an area of tundra, gradually changing to forest. Palaeolithic hunters may well have stalked the deer and ox which would have inhabited these woodlands, though no traces have yet been found of any settlements (some arrow flints have, however, been unearthed along the boundaries of the park in the south and north-east).

As someone fascinated by the early cave dwellers in France, I feel thwarted that no such evidence of Palaeolithic habitation has yet come to light in the limestone caverns along the southern fringes of the park. Perhaps, one day, a group of unsuspecting pot-holers will accidentally come across proof of an early occupation.

The distant mists of time become a little less

Rough grazing country on the slopes of the Black Mountain.

impenetrable with the advent of the Neolithic period from 5000 BC. Neolithic man, Britain's first farmer, began to modify and adapt the environment to his own needs by attacking the primeval forests that choked the land below around 2,000 feet. In so doing, Neolithic man initiated what has been called a 'centuries-long conversation between man and nature' concerning the evolution of landscape. Nothing, of course, remains of their timber-built settlements. Thankfully, for us, they also used stone, reserving this more durable building material for the tombs in which they buried their dead, thus indicating an interest in matters spiritual and eschatological which we, in our arrogance, often deny so-called 'primitive' man.

Whatever his motives, the stone tombs he constructed – based, according to one theory, on a practice brought to the Beacons by settlers from western France – were certainly built to last. A communal burial chamber, formed from large slabs and accessible by a walled passageway, would be covered by an earthen mound or long cairn of stones. In many cases, this protective covering has disappeared, leaving the basic framework of the tomb exposed to the skies, the stone slabs standing as cromlechs. A number of examples can be seen in the park, one of the best preserved being Ty Illtud. This small rectangular chamber, complete with ceiling-like 'capstone', stands in a field near Llanhamlach, a hamlet a few miles south-east of Brecon. Another fine example, easily viewed from the roadside on the north-western outskirts of Crickhowell, is known as Gwernvale, the remains of which have been excavated to reveal an elaborate

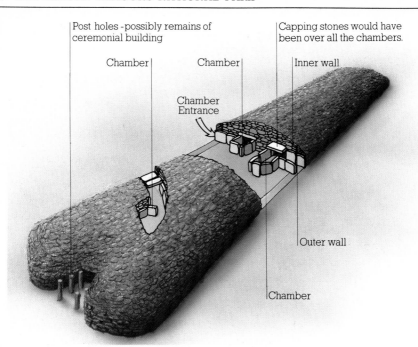

Post holes - possibly remains of ceremonial building

Chamber

Chamber

Chamber Entrance

Capping stones would have been over all the chambers.

Inner wall

Outer wall

Chamber

multi-tomb of four chambers. A third example, Ty Isaf, is located on private farmland almost four miles south of Talgarth. Its mound and upright stones are visible from the lane to the west of the field in which it stands.

How prehistoric man buried his dead: a reconstruction of the excavated Gwernvale long cairn near Crickhowell.

From around 2800 BC, Neolithic times evolved first into the Copper, and then the Bronze Ages. Man now had at his disposal more efficient metal tools and implements. The first major alterations to the Beacons' landscape thus took place as tree felling became much easier and ploughing much speedier than before. Bronze Age man may also have begun to farm and settle the upland areas. Certainly the use of these uplands as burial grounds is beyond doubt. By now, individual graves – round burial mounds of earth or stones – had largely replaced the longer communal chambered cairns of earlier times. These 'round barrows' are associated with the coming of the 'Beaker Folk', immigrants from the Continent. Chronologically, they bridge the gap between the end of Neolithic times and the beginning of the Bronze Age. This transitional group were so-called because of the shape of the ritual pottery vessels often found with their burials. Their graves are located most frequently on the higher ground in the park, one such cairn

Maen Llia, the solitary Bronze Age monolith in the fastness of Fforest Fawr.

appearing on the 2,863 ft (873 m) summit of Corn Du in the central Beacons.

High ground was also the favoured location for the most dramatic and mysterious of the park's prehistoric monuments: its standing stones and stone circles. No one, it seems, is ever likely to agree on the precise motives which inspired the construction of Stonehenge. Similarly, we are allowed to indulge in a little freewheeling speculation when we catch a glimpse, through the mists which so often shroud the lonely expanses of Fforest Fawr, of that solitary monolith, Maen Llia; and to let our imaginations run riot when confronted by the collection of stones known as Cerrig Duon (just over four miles west of Maen Llia) which, on first, erroneous impressions look like a random scattering across the high moorland.

Maen Llia is the park's best example of a single standing stone. Around twelve feet high by nine feet wide by two and a half feet thick, and tapering to a sharp point, this massive monolith at the head of the Llia valley may have been a monument to ancient spirits. A more prosaic explanation of its purpose relegates it to a mere route marker. Maen Llwyd, at the head of the Grwyne Fechan valley, is another fine example. Its truly remote location on rough moorland 1,880 ft (573 m) high on the flanks of Gadair Fawr makes it a site for the dedicated enthusiast only, who is not afraid of a little footslogging.

Whatever the truth of their origins, there are about thirty such stones to ponder over in the park, most of which are probably attributable to the Beaker Folk. Generally speaking, their main concentrations are to be found in the uplands around the Tawe valley and along the Vale of Usk. The mystery that has, for centuries, surrounded them has at least contributed to their survival. Legend and superstitious fear are most effective preservatives: an ancient Welsh law carried the penalty of death to anyone found harming the stones.

Stone circles, which date from around 2000 to 1300 BC, are approximate contemporaries of the single stone monuments. Cerrig Duon is possibly the best of the handful within the park. It can be seen from the minor mountain road running south from Trecastle to the A4067 near Craig-y-nos Country Park. This circle – to be more precise, it is egg shaped and, as such, is one of the few so far discovered in Britain – consists of short stones forming a perimeter of over 190 feet. Interestingly, a large standing stone known as Maen Mawr is positioned just outside the circle, with another about half a mile away to the north. Another intriguing feature is Cerrig Duon's relationship to a further collection of stones known as Saith Maen ('Seven Stones'). The seven are aligned in a row, pointing in the direction of Cerrig Duon three miles away in the next valley. To ascertain the purpose of these, and other stone monuments – megalithic calendars, ceremonial symbols, religious shrines, crude signposts, sun worshippers' temples, mystical meeting places or prehistoric parking lots? – you will have to ask the Beaker Folk.

Uncertainty also surrounds the park's most unconventional of prehistoric sites. The 'crannog', or artificial island, in Llangorse Lake can still be seen a little way offshore. Possibly dating from Iron Age times, this man-made island, consisting of a large mound of stones, would have supported a small number of dwellings. Fragments of pottery and a dug-out canoe have been found here, the latter (dated as late as AD 800) forming the centre-piece of an archaeological display at the Brecknock Museum in Brecon.

The most conspicuous of all prehistoric settlements are the hillforts which crown many a high point in the park. Many of them date from about 600 BC, when new influences from Europe brought the Iron Age to south Wales. The crossover from Bronze to Iron Age in these parts is summed up in a most spectacular fashion by the finds known as the Llyn Fawr Hoard. Along the shores of Llyn Fawr, a glacial lake just south of the park boundary near Hirwaun, newcomers to south Wales buried locally made bronze axes, an iron sword from the Continent, a cauldron, harness gear and other artefacts – possibly as offerings to the spirits. This remarkable collection of metal-work, numbering twenty-four objects in all, was discovered when the lake was adapted as a reservoir. Individual items are now on display at the National Museum of Wales in Cardiff.

A knowledge of iron-making was not the only major innovation that these immigrants brought with them. Within Wales, they enjoy a revered, mythological status as the people that probably introduced the Celtic language into Britain, a tongue that – according to the romantics, anyway – eventually evolved into Welsh, Cornish and Gaelic. These Celtic tribes also introduced a definite pattern of agricultural cultivation, continuing with the work of forest clearance in the sheltered valleys.

When it came to constructing their camps and settlements, however, their predilection was for the low hills and semi-uplands. Archaeologically, the Iron Age is best characterized by the sturdy hillforts which the Celtic tribes built in great abundance. These defended encampments served as secure strongholds for the tribesfolk and their cattle. Their pattern of distribution, on defensive sites above the best agricultural land in the park, suggests that the inhabitants would graze their flocks around the fort and cultivate the lower, more fertile grounds. Again, we can only guess at the primary function. Were they permanently inhabited or just a place of refuge during times of unrest? Were they market and trading centres, or built simply to discourage cattle thieves?

Although they occupy commanding positions, they did not – in comparison to the Roman forts and medieval castles of later eras – have a very wide sphere of influence or distinct strategic presence. The role of the Iron Age fort was in many cases limited to its immediate environs. Visitors to such powerful, wind-tossed sites as Garn Goch or Crug Hywel, can be forgiven for conjuring up images of

Plan of Garn Goch, the sprawling hillfort on the slopes of the Black Mountain.

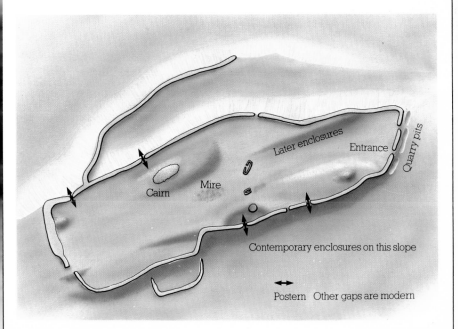

Later enclosures   Entrance   Quarry pits

Cairn   Mire

Contemporary enclosures on this slope

Postern   Other gaps are modern

Iron Age debris. The defences at Garn Goch, one of the largest Iron Age hillforts in Wales.

warlike tribes dominating a wide area from their lofty strongholds. Colourful legend takes another tumble in the face of informed opinion, which reveals the pedestrian realities of life during the Iron Age by declaring: 'Nor is there evidence that hillforts (in the Brecon Beacons) were the scene of serious assault, still less of sieges.'

None of this diminishes the monumental endeavour that must have gone into the construction of Garn Goch, one of the largest Iron Age hillforts in Wales. When I first visited this exposed, expansive site, the rain was attacking me horizontally; not really the ideal conditions in which to explore a fort that sprawls for thirty acres across elevated ground in the foothills of the wild Black Mountain.

Garn Goch on that day was much more a rain-lashed, sodden mound than the 'Red Mound' of its English translation, the name a possible reflection of the bracken which blazes bronze across the hillsides here each autumn. Ideal conditions or not, nothing could detract from the magnificence of the place. Previous experience of other Iron Age encampments had involved much searching for obscure signals of past occupation veiled beneath bracken or denuded by time, weather and the hand of man. Here, even the most sedentary or myopic of armchair archaeologists cannot fail to miss the evidence which, although over 2,000 years old, remains remarkably conspicuous.

The forest was a base for the Silures, a warlike tribe who dominated this part of south Wales prior to the Roman invasion (they also, incidentally, gave their name to one of the oldest rock types found in the area). Their great banks of stone defences, piled up in mounds of loose rubble, can still be seen to good effect (particularly on the west side), as can evidence of gateways and ditches. These outstanding remains are complemented by wonderful views northwards across the rolling pasturelands of the Tywi valley to the distant moors and conifer forests of mountainous mid-Wales.

The views from Crug Hywel ('Howell's Cairn') are even better. This small hillfort – shown as *Crucywel* on some maps – just about breaks the general rule by positioning itself at 1,481 ft (451 m) on the flat-topped spur above Crickhowell (for once it is quite obvious where the town inherited its name from!). The twenty-odd forts in the Beacons are usually on hills of moderate height and sited below 1,400 feet. Crug Hywel, a marginal exception, is a simple yet strong defensive point, preserving a single rampart, ditch and banking which follow the natural contours in a tear-drop shape.

Pen-y-crug, about a mile north-west of Brecon, is another fine site. In comparison with Crug Hywel's stark defences (probably early Iron Age), this is a later, more purposeful state-of-the-art hillfort. Well preserved and roughly oval in shape, Pen-y-crug covers five acres and is defended by a formidable series of four banks and ditches on most sides, with an annexe which may be a remnant of an earlier fort. My personal favourite though, is Castell Dinas at the head of the Rhiangoll valley, a few miles south of Talgarth. Another site to transgress the 1,400 foot rule (it is almost the same height as Crug Hywel), Castell Dinas stands as a lonely sentinel above a patchwork of fields but decidedly in the shadow of its towering neighbour, a massive spur of the Black Mountains. The fort's deep, grass-covered ditches and steep-sided ramparts look as if they are hundreds, not thousands of years old. The site is doubly interesting since it later caught the eye of medieval castle builders, who appreciated its naturally strategic position at the entrance to a narrow valley, though only fragmentary remains of their stone fortress now survive.

If these forts saw anything approaching active service, it would have been towards the end of the Iron Age with the coming of the Romans. The Romans' proud boast, *Veni, Vidi, Vici* ('I came, I saw, I conquered'), may well have applied in lowland Britain. When confronted by the belligerent Silures and the difficult, wooded upland terrain which they inhabited, their invasion machine shifted downwards a few gears. From the time they arrived in Britain in AD 43, it took them about twenty-five years to control and subdue their Welsh territories.

In the Beacons, they attempted to bring order by waging campaigns in the hills, constructing temporary camps along the way. One early Roman site in particular stimulates the imagination. Y Pigwn is today quite forgotten, its silence a strange counterpoint to the bustle and activity it must have witnessed almost 2,000 years ago when it was in the vanguard of the Roman conquest in this part of Wales.

This long-lost Roman camp is located on the Mynydd Bach Trecastell moorlands south-east of Llandovery. When I first went in search of this site, I missed it completely. Only second time around did I realize that the irregular mounds, bumps and hollows on the moor were imprints of a huge base which served as a temporary marching camp for legionary troops on the move against the fiercely resistant Silures. The camp, which was occupied only for short periods of time, was of sufficient size to accommodate an entire legion and its attendant auxiliaries.

Y Pigwn is sited at the western end of a well-preserved stretch of Roman road running across high ground between Trecastle and Llandovery (note the way in which it zig-zags down the hill just west of the camp in a series of carefully constructed terraces). Both road and camp are today ignored, effectively bypassed by the 'new' A40 route which runs in lower ground to the north.

The Brecon Beacons National Park is particularly fortunate in its wealth of well-preserved Roman trackways. Modern road-builders have sometimes taken advantage of routes forged by Romans, encasing in tarmacadam the foundation laid down by these accomplished early engineers. At other times, though – and these are the Roman routes to make for – the old military trackways lie, unused and unimproved, forging their typical, single-minded, 'as-the-crow-flies' way across moor and mountain.

Following in the tracks of the Romans? The spectacular 'Gap' route through the Brecon Beacons was possibly a Roman road.

Y Gaer is the key to our understanding of the Romans' network of roads in the Beacons. At Y Gaer (it translates simply as 'The Fort') a few miles west of Brecon, the Romans built for themselves an important base which served as linchpin in their long-term plans. By about AD 80, their conquest of Wales was more or less complete. To consolidate this victory, they built Y Gaer to house a garrison of 500 cavalry. By c. AD 140, the fort's original earth-and-timber defences had been replaced by stonework, enough of which survives to reveal its boxy, rectangular plan. Although military occupation probably lasted only until AD 200, the fort may have been used again from AD 300, possibly as a civilian settlement.

Y Gaer is an incongruous site. What was once an influential Roman power base now lies, almost totally ignored, in a farmer's field above a peaceful loop in the River Usk. However, its convergent role in defining the Romans' network of communications in these parts was crucial. All roads led to Y Gaer. The route to the west, via Y Pigwn, connected Y Gaer with another fort at Llandovery. Forts at Neath and Coelbren were linked to Y Gaer by a well-engineered trackway across the wastes of Fforest

The Roman fort of Y Gaer stands in farmland west of Brecon.

Fawr. The camp at Penydarren, Merthyr Tydfil, had its north-south link across the Beacons – although the famous 'Gap' trackway which takes advantage of a 1,961 ft (598 m) break in the summit ridge to breach the Beacons above the Neuadd reservoirs, so often assumed to be of Roman origin, may be nothing of the kind. A route to the south-east from Y Gaer would have travelled along the Usk valley to Abergavenny, Usk itself and the major legionary base at Caerleon, whilst there was also probably a northbound road to Castell Collen at Llandrindod Wells.

Undoubtedly, the best stretch of Roman road in the park is the Sarn Helen trackway linking Coelbren to Y Gaer. Long sections of original road, unbroken and uninterrupted for quite a few miles, traverse largely uninhabited moorland in a south-western corner of the park. This exhilarating route is made even more interesting due to its encounter, along the way, with Maen Madoc, an ancient stone which stands by the roadside on an exposed, windy crest a little way from Sarn Helen's junction with the minor mountain road north of Ystradfellte. This slender pillar stone, about nine feet high, is a fascinating example of the way in which Roman and Celtic cultures inevitably mixed. The inscription, in Latin, dates from after the Roman occupation and was probably made on an existing plain standing stone. It has been translated as '[The stone] of Dervacus, son of Justus. He lies here'.

The Romans finally left Britain after AD 400, their empire in ruins. It is unlikely that the 300-odd years of Roman occupation were ones of continual strife. An uneasy peace must have prevailed in the south Wales highlands where, in contrast to the more

One of the few landmarks in Fforest Fawr: Maen Madoc, the inscribed standing stone beside a well-preserved stretch of the Sarn Helen Roman road.

The original 'Llywel Stone' now resides in the British Museum, but a cast of this ancient inscribed stone can be seen in Llywel Church and the Brecknock Museum.

amenable lowland areas of Britain, the Romans made few efforts to introduce a more civilized life-style by building towns and villas, though we know there was a villa at Llanfrynach (now destroyed) and evidence exists of dwellings around Y Gaer. Quite probably, the native Celts, after the first shock of conquest, went about their lives much as before.

The Brecknock Museum contains a marvellous collection of Roman artefacts. Carved stones, pottery, tiles, jewellery and coins are all on display, as are items relating to the most significant historical development in the two centuries after the Roman departure – Wales's conversion to Christianity. If times had been hard under the rule of Rome, they were even more difficult after the withdrawal of the imperial eagle standard. The Romans had, at least, imposed a sense of order. One somewhat partisan nineteenth-century historian has written comparing the Romans quite favourably with the new wave of Saxon invaders who followed in their wake. This 'savage and cruel fair-headed, blue-eyed race' were, he stated, 'very different'. These newcomers 'poured into the Welsh provinces, beating their shields with their spears, and calling on the wild birds to eat of the feast of their providing'.

The only glimmers of light in the chaotic Dark Ages came from the Celtic missionaries who travelled the land preaching the message of Christianity. Memorial stones and sculptured crosses at the Brecknock Museum are reminders of these times, though better still are the churches, scattered across the park, whose roots go back to the early Christian era.

At Llangorse, for example, a place of worship was established sometime around the sixth century by St

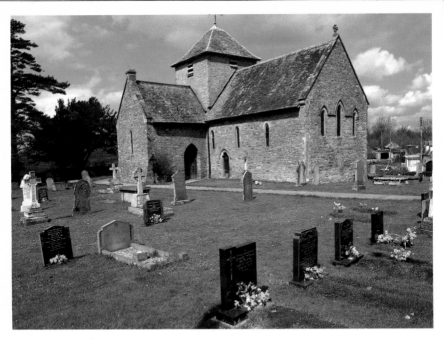

Paulinus, tutor to St David, Wales's patron saint. The present church, dedicated to Paulinus, can be traced back to the community of monks he founded here. Additional evidence of this church's pre-medieval roots takes the form of a Viking burial stone uncovered on the site. Llanddew, a mile or two north-east of Brecon, is another ancient settlement. Its church of St David (*Dewi Sant* in Welsh) was first mentioned as a religious site in AD 500. Llangattock, like Llanddew and so many other towns and villages, embodies in its place-name its early religious connections (*Llan* meaning 'church' or 'enclosure'). In Llangattock's case, it refers to St Catwg, a Celtic holy man – and contemporary of St David's – who died in about AD 577.

The tiny isolated church at Llanddeusant is built on the site of another monastery connected with St Paulinus. Again, there exists corroborating evidence of its great antiquity – this time in the shape of a cross slab possibly dating from between the seventh and ninth centuries, recently discovered near the church. Mynydd Illtud, the grassy common west of Brecon, is named after St Illtud who, with St David, was the most influential of the early Christian teachers. Illtud, founder of the

The village of Llanddew is ranged around — and named after — its church of St David, one of the oldest religious sites in the area.

important monastic settlement at Llantwit Major
c. AD 500, was traditionally thought to be buried on
the common at Bedd Illtud, a site marked by a
collection of large stones in a shallow pit (it is now
believed his body lies elsewhere, possibly at
Llantwit Major).

The most evocative religious site of all, on the
strength of its other-worldly, mountain-locked
location deep in the Black Mountains, is Llanthony (a
place 'truly calculated for religion' according to the
medieval chronicler Giraldus Cambrensis, the
Archdeacon of Brecon who lived at Llanddew for
much of his life). The ruined priory founded here in
1118 is a relative newcomer, for it occupies the site
of a much earlier chapel. This chapel, dedicated to
St David, pre-dates the priory by 600 years and
gives Llanthony its name (a corruption of the Welsh
Llanddewi nant honddu, 'The church of St David on
the River Honddu').

As well as a nascent Christianity, the fifth and sixth
centuries also saw the emergence of Brycheiniog, a
princedom which corresponds very closely to
today's park boundaries (the only real exception
occurring in the Black Mountain). In establishing a
separate distinctive geographical entity,
Brycheiniog's influence has been extremely
pervasive. The name Brecknock, or the 'old' county
title Breconshire, are both Anglicized equivalents to
Brycheiniog. Officially, the name may have lost
some of its status when the area became
incorporated into the vast new super-county of
Powys during local government reorganization in
1974. In practice, it is still as relevant as ever
amongst the locals (ask anyone who reads the
Brecon and Radnor Express), for, quite apart from
deep-seated tradition, Brecknock has been retained
as a district borough and, although borough and
park boundaries are different, Brecknock's
continued identity is further reinforced by the
existence of the Brecon Beacons National Park.

The princedom took its name from Brychan, a
fifth-century chieftain of Irish ancestry and
progenitor of a powerful ruling dynasty. He looms
large out of the mists that shroud the obscure Dark
Ages as an influential figure and creator of a
political unit which probably survived as an
independent realm up until the tenth century. This
longevity might partly be due to an abundance of
descendants: according to legend, Brychan had a
family of no less than eleven sons and twenty-five
daughters, many of whom led religious lives. Fact

The rose-tinged
stonework at Llanthony's
old priory preserves
many fine examples of
ecclesiastic architectural
detail.

and fiction sometimes collide, the former reinforcing the latter. In Brychan's case, his familial influence is underlined by the gravestones discovered in the Beacons, some bearing telling inscriptions in the Irish-influenced Ogham script, or Latin, or even both. Additional evidence comes from their distribution, clearly within the eastern, western and southern boundaries of the ancient princedom.

During the Dark Ages, other boundaries were also being defined, most notably the first official border between what we now know as Wales and England. This assumed the form of the huge earthen dyke constructed in the eighth century by King Offa of Mercia. A long distance footpath now follows the line of the original dyke, wherever possible, from south to north Wales. Good stretches of this 168 mile path run along the eastern boundary of the park in the hills directly above Llanthony and the Vale of Ewyas.

Brycheiniog, then, was a well-established separate entity at the approach of medieval times and the coming of the Normans. As with the Romans before them, their 'conquest' was far more tentative in the hostile uplands than in the less challenging lowland Britain. A troubled period in the park's history, lasting for two centuries, began soon after the famous date of 1066. Initially, the Norman invaders constructed castles of earth and timber. These crude motte-and-bailey strongholds, quick and cheap to put up, soon appeared at strategic points in valleys and passes, controlling and containing the natives in the hillier country. These castles were the work of Bernard de Neufmarché, the Norman baron (and, incidentally, William the Conqueror's half-brother) who was instrumental in the conquest of Brycheiniog.

He constructed strongholds at Hay, Bronllys and Talgarth (in 1088) and, after he had defeated and killed Brycheiniog's native ruler, at Brecon itself (in the early 1090s). Other castles followed, initially built to the motte-and-bailey design which could be put up in just over a week. The motte was a steep earthen mound with a timber tower, surrounded by a palisade. The bailey, adjoining the motte, was an earthwork enclosure, also usually defended by a wooden rampart and ditch. Trecastle's tree-covered mound, on the eastern approach to the village and quite clearly man-made, is a good example even though it has suffered almost a millennium of neglect.

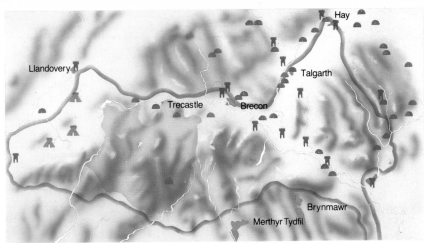

The medieval scene in the Brecon Beacons.

〜 National Park Boundary

Great Forest of Brecknock

🗡 Main stone castles

⬣ Lesser castles/mounds

⬡ Castle site

🏯 Welsh Manors

In later Norman times, impermanent timber defences were superseded by solid masonry. Many mottes were strengthened through the construction of stone keeps and walls. Bronllys is a classic example of this evolution in castle design. Its single round tower, perched like a massive stone chimney on top of a steep conical hill, is a thirteenth-century addition to an eleventh-century motte. Only battered shells and fragments remain of the stone castles at Crickhowell, Hay, Llandovery and the aforementioned Castell Dinas.

Blaen-Camlais, on Mynydd Illtud near the Brecon Beacons Mountain Centre, is a pronounced mound topped by a pile of stones: all that is left of a round tower that was once some fifty feet tall. This site is unusual in that it may well have been a castle built by the native Welsh – in this case, Llywelyn ap Gruffudd (Llywelyn the Last) – as opposed to the Norman newcomers.

The park's outstanding castle also has an unconventional pedigree, having served both as an English fortification and native stronghold. Carreg Cennen Castle stands unchallenged, head and shoulders above the rest, including most of the 400-odd military medieval sites in Wales.

This stumpy ruin has, in its time, been held, retaken and held again by Welsh and English forces. Little wonder, then, that its walls and towers are far from immaculate, though the elements must also have played their destructive part for the castle stands, vulnerable to wind and rain, on top of an exposed 300 foot limestone outcrop in the foothills of the Black Mountain.

Despite – or possibly because of – its tumbledown aura, Carreg Cennen is now beginning to gain just recognition as one of Britain's truly stirring castles. More visitors are now taking the trouble to seek out this off-the-beaten-track medieval site, located amongst the back lanes just over four miles south-east of Llandeilo. This dramatic fortress, with its complicated system of defences built into the side of a vertical cliff, has the rare ability to evoke an authentic medieval spirit. And not everything stands above ground. A narrow doorway in the corner of the courtyard leads down into a 230 foot passageway cut right into the cliff face which ends in a cave, beneath the castle foundations, in which prehistoric skeletons have been discovered. If you only have time to visit one castle in south Wales, be sure to choose Carreg Cennen.

Militarily, the most important of the park's medieval castles was the one built in Brecon. Today, with one part of the old fortress integrated into the fabric of an hotel, and one of the towers unceremoniously cut off by a road which drives right through the middle of the site, it is difficult to accept that this was the principal power base from which the Normans controlled their new lordship of

Carreg Cennen Castle, unquestionably one of the most spectacularly sited medieval fortresses in Wales, crowns a rocky outcrop in the foothills of the Black Mountain.

Brecon. The predictably named Castle Hotel has managed to graft itself on to quite substantial sections of medieval stonework whilst, across the road in private grounds, stands the dismembered twelfth-century keep known as the Ely Tower.

The medieval churches in the Brecon Beacons have stood the test of time far more successfully than their contemporary military sites. Many parish

Woodcarving at its most accomplished. The outstanding Tudor rood screen at Partrishow church, one of the finest in Wales.

Take a torch and explore this dramatic vaulted passageway, cut into the cliff face at Carreg Cennen Castle, which leads to a cave beneath the fortress's foundations.

churches in the park boast long and fascinating histories, together with beautiful architectural features such as finely crafted stonework and intricate woodcarvings. Partrishow church, in particular, has an exceptional rood screen, dating from early Tudor times. Possibly the best example in Wales, it is fashioned from Irish oak to a standard that speaks volumes of the painstaking skill and attention to detail displayed by the ecclesiastical woodcarver. Other interesting features in this fascinating church include an eleventh-century font and macabre wall painting of a skeleton – brandishing spade, scythe and hourglass – depicting death.

Two sites in the park deserve special attention on the strength of their roles as major religious centres, past and present. The shell of Llanthony Priory, already mentioned in connection with its early Christian roots, leaves us in no doubt that this was once an important monastic community. Giraldus Cambrensis added to his observations on the place by writing that Llanthony was 'more adapted to canonical discipline than all the monasteries of the British Isles'.

As a priory, Llanthony really dates from the early

Hotel or medieval castle? Brecon's Castle Hotel, built into the ruined fabric of the town's ancient fortress, has been tastefully extended and renovated.

twelfth century when the Norman knight, William de Lacy, discovered the earlier chapel here. Immediately captivated, he renounced all worldly pursuits and established a hermitage here which grew into an Augustinian priory. Llanthony's greatest architectural glory is its row of pointed transitional archways which look out on to remote border country that can have changed comparatively little in the priory's 800 year history. What would the abbots have thought, though, about the unique little hotel-cum-pub built into the priory ruins? (One word of advice: the priory is often confused with yet another Llanthony, at Capel-y-ffin about three miles to the north. Here, the charismatic nineteenth-century religious figure, Father Ignatius, built a short-lived monastery – later the home of artist Eric Gill – which he called Llanthony Abbey.)

Brecon Cathedral, on the hill above the town, serves the Diocese of Swansea and Brecon. Although assuming its current cathedral status as recently as 1923, it is an ancient site, founded along with its next-door castle by Bernard de Neufmarché, originally as a priory. As it now stands, the cathedral is basically a fourteenth-century structure much restored and rebuilt over the years. Large, solid and somewhat squat, it is more impressive within than its exterior appearance suggests. The cathedral's richly furnished interior is particularly noteworthy for its fine Early English chancel arch, impressive vaulting and thirteenth-century choir in front of a magnificently sculpted reredos.

A walled town grew up around Bernard de Neufmarché's castle and priory. Norman Brecon thus became an important seat of power, though its

Llanthony Priory's archways frame a tranquil, timeless scene.

Good farmland in the sheltered Usk valley near Abergavenny.

influence in practical terms was not as great as might be supposed. As with the Romans before them, the Normans did not wring large-scale changes out of the native Welsh. For a start, the alien concept of townships was inimical to country folk. Brecon, one suspects, was a place to be avoided at all costs.

Neither did the basic pattern of farming change all that much. The Normans' manorial system had features in common with native Welsh agricultural practices, at least as far as the rugged higher country was concerned. English and Welsh manors shared grazing rights on the common pasture that is still, even today, a widespread feature in the mountainous areas of the park. Indeed, the Normans appear to have taken a rather sanguine attitude to the hillier country in the east and centre of the Beacons, where indigenous Welsh manors and customs were allowed to prevail as long as rents were forthcoming. The same applied to almost all of the western half of the park, where established Welsh ways continued to flourish.

The eastern lowlands saw the greatest changes. Here, on the better arable land, the Normans introduced a feudal system of farming. Tenants worked directly for the lord of the manor, tending his crops and animals, in marked contrast to the more independent arrangements on the local higher grounds and lands further west. The pattern of farming thus established by both Normans and Welshmen still prevails in the park today: the empty, open areas of unenclosed common pasture in the high mountains; the scattered hill farming and occasional hamlets found below about 1,000 feet, particularly in the west of the park; and the settled, more fertile lowlands along the Usk and Llynfi valleys in the east where the Normans influence really took hold and where villages are mainly manorial in origin.

During medieval times, woodland clearance continued in the valleys and lower uplands, stimulated by an appetite for more and more arable land. One area, an inviolate 'place apart' from all the rest, was Fforest Fawr, the 'Great Forest' of Brecknock. Misconceptions habitually surround this part of the park. Fforest Fawr is not – and was not – a 'forest' as defined by our understanding of the word. It might have been tree-clad in prehistoric times, though this would have had no bearing on its name. Its etymology has medieval roots, when the

Tretower's stone keep, dating from the twelfth century, is only half of the story of this fascinating two-in-one historic site. Across the field stands Tretower Court, a handsome, fortified manor house built in the more peaceful late middle ages.

term 'forest' was used to describe an area of land used as a hunting ground.

Fforest Fawr was, in fact, a royal hunting ground. In the higher parts it would have looked much as it does today, a landscape of bare moor and mountainside over 1,500 feet high for large stretches but with settlements in the wooded valleys. At its greatest extent in the Middle Ages it included all the land between the Usk in the north and the Pyrddin and Mellte in the south, and from the Carmarthen Fans eastwards to the Tarell. From later medieval times, the forest's role as a hunting ground declined. Agricultural activity increased, sheep and cattle were grazed on its common pasture, replacing the deer and wild boar previously hunted here, whilst tenant farmers grew corn in the better valley land.

These were more peaceful, settled times for Wales, as the strife of the earlier medieval period gradually ran its course. One monument in the Brecon Beacons neatly sums up this decline in conflict. Tretower Court and Castle is a fascinating two-in-one historic site which charts, in its architecture, the evolution from warlike to relatively peaceful times in these parts. A stark, round tower, unequivocally military in design, stands next to a handsome fortified manor house which must have been a comfortable residence of its era. The contrasts are vivid: the tower, built within an earlier rectangle of stone defences, remains as an icon to the bellicose twelfth and thirteenth centuries, whilst the court, dating from the late fourteenth and fifteenth centuries, reflects the ascendancy of home comforts over military considerations.

3 **The last few centuries**

To express concern about the survival of the Brecon Beacons as an unspoilt stretch of countryside would have been unthinkable even as recently as a few hundred years ago. As medieval times gave way to the sixteenth and seventeenth centuries, 'man's impact on his surroundings,' to quote one authority, 'remained so marginal that the wilderness seemed all pervasive'. Under such circumstances, conservation would have been as alien a concept as space travel, theme parks and fast food. 'Natural' scenery meant little, if anything, to the sixteenth-century mind. Beauty was only perceived to exist in formal, orderly surroundings – such as neat, precisely planned gardens – where nature had been tamed and brought to heel by the hand of man.

The giant steps of Sgwd Clun-gwyn ('White Meadow Fall') on the River Mellte south of the Porth yr Ogof Cave.

How different it became a few hundred years later. The Rev. H Elvet Lewis, who gave us the

benefit of his nineteenth-century observations earlier in the book at the start of the geology section, was all the more flattering towards the Brecon Beacons because of the distance they maintained from man's influence. His appreciation was quite obviously heightened when he wrote of Pen y Fan as 'this loftiest elevation of South Wales [that] towers in loneliness . . . thus having a good chance to keep the fumes of iron-furnaces and collieries at a respectable distance'. By this time, man's perceptions were beginning to turn full circle. In the harsh new light of industry and technology, the elemental majesty of nature, untainted by man, became a major artistic preoccupation celebrated by painters and poets.

Within this new awareness of nature lay the seeds of Britain's national parks, as well as the officially designated 'areas of outstanding natural beauty' and other protected stretches of countryside and coastline. The Brecon Beacons provides us with a most illuminating case history into our changing attitudes towards wild and lonely landscapes. The mountains here were once viewed as downright unpleasant; the romantic spirit, for example, was yet to seduce the likes of Daniel Defoe who, in 1724,

Bygone brickworks at Penwyllt. The brick kilns here were last fired up in the inter-war years.

described the Beacons as 'horrid and frightful, even worse than those mountains abroad'. Are these the same Beacons which now give so much pleasure to so many?

New circumstances breed new perceptions. The onset of large-scale industrialization swept away old values. In landscape terms, man the benevolent gardener became man the destroyer. In south

Wales, of course, iron-making and coal mining swiftly became dominant forces; yet the Brecon Beacons, although next-door neighbour to this industrial explosion, escaped exceedingly lightly. Apart from some incursions into the southern fringe of the park, industry kept to its side of the fence, confining itself to the burgeoning coal-mining valleys.

The profound, devastating effects of the Industrial Revolution – the greatest changer of landscapes since the introduction of agrarian methods in Neolithic times – were felt only in concentrated points along the southern fringes of the Brecon Beacons. In military terms, the two sides line up as the immutable Old Red Sandstone scenery to the north versus the tumultuous, teeming southern coalfield, no-man's-land being conveniently defined for us today by the east-west A465 'Heads of the Valleys' road between Abergavenny and Glynneath.

Prior to the Industrial Revolution the park had seen a few isolated experiments with the new technology of the times. These occurred in the south-western and south-eastern fringes of the Beacons, where the availability of the raw materials necessary for iron-making – iron ore, limestone and wood, together with swift streams to power the bellows – led to the establishment of charcoal-fired blast furnaces in the sixteenth century. By and large, though, things went on much as before. The local economy here continued to be an agrarian-based one involving both pastoral and arable farming but with particular emphasis on sheep rearing and the wool trade. Cloth was made domestically and at small, water-powered woollen mills and grain was ground at flour mills in an area where the patterns of work and life were still determined by the cycle of the seasons.

The Brecon Beacons were not completely immunized against the upheavals taking place to the south. As the Industrial Revolution gained momentum, rural folk migrated in substantial numbers to work in the foundries and mines, leaving in their wake abandoned farmsteads and untended land, particularly in the park's western and eastern mountains. Limestone quarries began to appear along the southern Carboniferous belt to satisfy the demands of local iron-works. Gouged outcrops, scooped skylines and greyish-white cliffs, leftovers from past quarrying activity, are a common sight along the southern limestone belt

Industry mellowed by the passage of time. Remains of early industrial activity in the wooded Clydach gorge, once a thriving iron-smelting centre.

(most notably in the crags just north of Merthyr Tydfil, once the iron- and steel-producing 'capital' of the world, and above Llangattock). This quarrying still continues today within the park, though it is now concentrated at five locations (one of the largest, at Vaynor, is mostly excluded by a 'loop' in the park boundary).

Limestone was also hewn from the sides of the Clydach gorge. This deep vale was the scene of very early iron smelting which pre-dated the Industrial Revolution by nearly 200 years. This infant industrial activity took hold most tenaciously within the thickly wooded gorge, its handful of seventeenth-century charcoal-burning forges laying the foundations for a number of coke-fired blast furnaces in the eighteenth and nineteenth centuries. The gorge represents the only real major, concentrated industrial incursion in the park, and as such is a magnet for those interested in this period. The full complement of industrial and social forces were at work here, for in addition to the quarries, coal was mined in adits (tunnels dug into the steep hillsides following the line of the coal seams), tramways and railways were laid down, bridges and lime kilns built and workers' housing put up.

The spark has long since departed from this industrial community. Today, the Clydach gorge is disturbed only by the sound of vehicles as they drive through this natural gateway into the valleys on the A465. For the best overall view of the gorge and its industrial remains take one of the minor roads which run on the higher ground to the north of the busy Heads of the Valleys route. The panoramas are not of a desolate industrial moonscape. The woods here must have been too abundant even for those most dedicated choppers-down-of-trees, the charcoal burners, for Clydach's surviving woodland cover is surprisingly extensive. The gorge, in fact, contains what is thought to be one of the few native beechwoods – now a national nature reserve – surviving in Wales.

The Industrial Revolution was but one of the far-reaching forces to affect eighteenth-century society. The other was religion, which, in parts of Wales at least, matched in its spiritual intensity the physical changes wrought by the new industrial age. If Wales's Nonconformist religious movement, and the Methodist Revival that it spawned, has a birthplace, then it must be Maesyronen. Wales's reputation as a chapel-going, hymn-singing country can be traced back to this early place of worship, located just outside the park between Hay and Glasbury.

Tiny Maesyronen, looking more like a farmer's barn than a prototype for the heroically proportioned chapels which dominate many a Welsh village, is tucked away from the world's gaze on a country lane above the Wye valley. It was built in about 1696 in this deliberately discreet, out-of-the-way spot so that religious dissenters could meet here in secret, under the cover of darkness. The atmospheric old chapel is still in use today, and preserves a remarkable interior with furniture dating back to the eighteenth century.

One of the Methodist Revival's most influential – and certainly most interesting – leaders was Howell Harris (1714–73). He is forever associated with Trefeca, a hamlet between Llangorse and Talgarth, where he established a religious community – in many ways an early version of a kibbutz or commune – known as 'The Family' or 'Connexion', the members of which pooled their resources for the common good. A fascinating man of many talents, and apparently master of them all, he was also a pioneer printer and accomplished agriculturalist. Harris founded the Brecknockshire Agricultural Society in 1755, the first of its kind in Wales, and helped introduce many of the latest machines and improvements in agriculture to this part of the country (he is even credited with introducing Welsh farmers to the turnip!).

But it was in his role as a charismatic evangelical preacher that he is best remembered. Following his famous vision at Talgarth church in 1735, where he 'felt suddenly my heart melting like before a fire,

The chapel at Capel-y-ffin in the secluded Vale of Ewyas, a borderland valley noted for its religious sites.

with love to God my Saviour', he became an indefatigable advocate, preaching to gatherings large and small, anywhere and everywhere, from his mobile pulpit. The community which he founded, now a Presbyterian college, contains a little museum dedicated to this extraordinary, multi-talented man.

William Williams, Pantycelyn (1717–91), was also an important religious figure. 'Pantycelyn', part-and-parcel of his name, was the title of the farm – still standing – in which he lived about three miles east of Llandovery. Converted after hearing a sermon by Harris at Talgarth, he travelled through Wales as an itinerant preacher. His hymn-writing talents have earned him a place in posterity. Possibly the greatest of all Welsh religious composers ('Guide me, O Thou Great Jehovah' – originally written in Welsh – is the best known of his many works), his hymns played a vital role in spreading the Methodist Revival across eighteenth-century Wales.

In the following years the most important change on the ground in the Brecon Beacons was the enclosure of Fforest Fawr, the 'Great Forest', a process initiated by the Enclosure Act of 1815. The arcane laws of the forest, a former royal hunting ground, were swept aside by Act of Parliament during the first part of the nineteenth century. The lower and peripheral land was sold off, and the remainder divided between the Commoners and the Crown.

These events coincided with a marked escalation in sheep farming throughout south Wales's hill country to a position of major importance, an increase stimulated by the growing demand for mutton and wool from the new industrial regions, the introduction of more productive breeds of sheep and the shortages experienced during and after the Napoleonic Wars. Even before the period of enclosures in the Brecon Beacons from 1815 to 1819, the sheep flocks were on the increase in Fforest Fawr. The most significant development of all, though, was the introduction of large-scale farming to the region. Some commoners improved the numbers and quality of their flocks by renting land from other owners to create large acreages. The sale of the Crown allotment, and its subsequent leasing in the mid-nineteenth century to the Cnewr Company as a single unit, created by far the biggest sheep farm – 'ranch' would be a better description – of them all. This vast acreage created the scope necessary for the introduction of sheep farming on very extensive and commercial lines (the Cnewr Estate still exists and is, in some senses, today's successor to the original 'Great Forest': it is the one large upland area in the park to which public access is not freely available).

In charting the developments in Welsh hill-sheep farming – at least as far as the Brecon Beacons are concerned – credit must also be given to Scottish

Sheep still roam the barren wastes of Fforest Fawr. Flocks are gathered together in these pens close to the encroaching conifer, a sign of changing times and land use.

A long-abandoned trackway in the foothills of the Black Mountain near Carreg Cennen Castle.

influences. The Cnewr Company was founded by a Scotsman, one of the many enterprising nineteenth-century immigrants (mainly from Ayrshire) to settle in Fforest Fawr and make a great contribution locally by raising the general standards of both meat and wool through introducing the hardy Cheviot breed to cross with Welsh stock. In the north-east of Fforest Fawr, for example, the area now known as Forest Lodge – originally called Llosged but renamed by its new owner – was another to increase its flocks under Scottish influence. The extensive pasturages which thus arose from the sale or enclosure of Fforest Fawr – and the new lifeblood attracted to this area – resulted in Breconshire becoming one of Wales's leading sheep-rearing counties by the end of the century, with a sheep population approaching half a million.

The farming community also benefited from other changes, in the form of better communications. First came the toll-charging turnpike roads introduced into this area from 1767. The mountainous, sparsely populated Beacons were never afflicted by the 'road mania' which struck so many parts of Britain. Here, it was a case of quality rather than quantity,

A road to nowhere. An ancient pathway between disused agricultural dwellings in the sparsely populated Black Mountain.

the turnpikes forming the basis for many of today's main arteries of communication through the park.

The snaking A4069 which traverses the Black Mountain, for instance, was originally a turnpike road, dating from 1790, on which farmers transported lime from the Amman to the Tywi valley. Other turnpikes linked Brecon with Merthyr Tydfil and also the Neath and Tawe valleys. An early turnpike road following the Roman original across Mynydd Bach Trecastell's high ground between Llandovery and Trecastle was replaced, in the first part of the nineteenth century, by a sheltered valley road to the north, the current A40.

The A40 runs right across the northern section of the park from Abergavenny to Llandeilo. In the days of the stagecoach this route, a section of the important link between London and Milford Haven, was a thoroughfare busy with fast stages. It is still a favourite road for traffic heading into and out of west Wales, so much so that the old stagecoaches could probably keep up with the slow-moving convoys of cars and caravans that often choke this route on busy summer weekends, though the situation has eased with the opening of the M4 and, more recently, Brecon's bypass.

Many old pubs and hotels along the way clearly display their ancestry as inns and staging posts where the coaches would take on passengers and mail, and also change horses. One of the best examples is the Bear Hotel, located right on a bend in the roadside as the A40 weaves through the pretty little town of Crickhowell. Externally, its cobbled courtyard and entrance arch, still decorated with the words 'Post Horses', give the game away. Within the cosy bar hangs an old notice which provides more evidence of the hotel's past role. Dated 1852, it states that the Brecon, London and Carmarthen stages depart daily at seven am, though those unfortunate enough to have to travel to Gloucester need to be here, ready and waiting, at the unearthly hour of one-fifty am (Sundays excepted, of course).

A journey by stagecoach, to late twentieth-century romantics, is no doubt a whimsical, appealing prospect. In practice, the trip would have been tiring, bone-shaking, and sometimes downright dangerous. Further along the A40, as it winds its way through the narrow, wooded valley between Trecastle and Llandovery, a roadside obelisk near the hamlet of Halfway reminds us that coach passengers had their share of accidents. The obelisk, known as the 'Coachman's Cautionery' or 'Mail Coach Pillar', was possibly the first traffic warning signal to be erected in Wales. It was put up in memory of a coach, loaded with passengers, which was driven over the edge at this point in 1835 by a drunken driver. Its inscription tells how it was 'erected as a caution to mail coach drivers to keep from intoxication'. The accident sounds horrific, for we learn that the driver, Edward Jenkins, 'was intoxicated at the time and drove the mail on the wrong side of the road and going at full speed or gallop met a cart ... and went down over the precipice 121 feet where ... the coach was dashed into several pieces'. You have been warned.

A journey along a placid inland waterway was altogether a far less frenetic affair. Canals were the next transportation 'mania' to grip Britain. Their role, as the first transport servants of the Industrial Revolution, was a crucial one, and in the Brecon Beacons led to the construction of the Monmouthshire and Brecon Canal. Built between 1797 and 1812 to link Brecon with Newport and the Severn estuary, it was the final component in a transportation system which carried produce, initially by tramway and then by barge, from nearby

Walk beside the towpath—or better still, cruise along the Monmouthshire and Brecon Canal.

mines and quarries. The canal also served a small local iron-works and carried other goods such as domestic coal, timber, wool and food.

Hardly had canals been established than a third 'mania' – for rail transport – swept all before it. Canal traffic soon declined and by the twentieth century the Monmouthshire and Brecon waterway had fallen into disuse. Following restoration, it was re-opened in 1970 for navigation between Brecon and Pontymoile (near Pontypool), a distance of thirty-two miles. Its industrial roots are not easily traced. The only British canal to run entirely within a national park, it charts a languid, highly scenic route along the pastoral Usk valley. Designed to follow the contours of the landscape, it has long since blended beautifully into the hillside on which it was cut. Little wonder that it now enjoys a new lease of life as an inland waterway popular with holiday cruisers (with main boat-hire centres at Gilwern and Govilon), even though the canal is prone to occasional breaches which sometimes prevent continual navigation along its entire length.

Talybont is one of the places which bear traces of the canal's former utilitarian purpose. Remains of old lime kilns still stand on the canalside here, reminders of the time when limestone was brought by tramway to this once-thriving hub of communications from the Trefil quarries to the south-west. A complex network of abandoned tramways criss-crosses the southern fringes of the park. The industries in the Clydach gorge were connected to the canal by a tramway running to Gilwern. Another particularly impressive old tramroute ran through rocky, difficult terrain past

The narrow-gauge Brecon Mountain Railway runs from the northern edge of Merthyr Tydfil to a scenic lakeside terminus in the foothills of the Beacons.

towering Craig y Ddinas (Dinas Rock) at Pontneddfechan, linking a silica mine to the Vale of Neath Canal. These abandoned industrial trackways today make fascinating footpaths-with-a-difference, the qualities of which were hauntingly captured in Alexander Cordell's famous novel, *Rape of the Fair Country*. This is set around what is now a south-eastern corner of the park, and a journey by tram was described in the following way: 'The loveliness of God's earth comes into you; its beauty new in the phantom shapes of trees in moonlight.'

Victorian society's display of heroic optimism – or possibly blind folly – is best expressed in its addiction to railways. No challenge was too great to the Victorian engineer, no speculation too risky for the Victorian financier. As in other parts of Britain, the 'Age of Steam' produced, in the Brecon Beacons, rail routes that were testaments to the skills of the technicians who built them if not the commercial instincts of the companies that funded them.

One classic, though hardly profitable, railway – surely amongst Britain's most scenic prior to its closure in 1962 – was the Merthyr Tydfil to Brecon line. Opened in 1863, it climbed through the mountain-ringed Taf Fechan and Talybont valleys on some severely challenging gradients. At remote Torpantau (the lone signal box here, now demolished, stood at well over 1,000 feet), the mountains proved too much even for the intrepid railway engineers, who were forced to dig a long tunnel in order to negotiate the summit. Other railways, also victims of the 1962 closures, connected Brecon with Hay and Neath. Thanks to the Brecon Mountain Railway, we can at least

experience a brief taste of the scenic delights these old rail routes gave their passengers. This narrow-gauge line, one of the 'Great Little Trains of Wales', is laid along part of the old Merthyr to Brecon route. It currently runs from a terminus at Pant (just north of Merthyr) for about two miles to a lakeside halt at Pontsticill, though there are plans to extend it further along the valley.

The twentieth, more than any previous century, easily accounts for the greatest physical changes within the park. The landscape has been irrevocably altered by modifying forces which can be summed up in two words: water and wood. Man-made reservoirs and conifer forest are now an unavoidable – and some would say overly intrusive and ill-fitting – piece of the picture here, especially along the south-facing slopes of the park. There are, for example, no less than eighteen direct supply reservoirs in the park or along its boundaries, covering around 1,500 acres of land in all. The reasons behind this wealth of water are simple: it rains a lot here (up to 100 inches a year on the higher ground) and there are plenty of valleys deep enough to be dammed. The Beacons, then, could have been purpose-built for their role in quenching

Broad-leaf almost meets conifer near the headwaters of the Talybont reservoir.

the thirst of the highly populated urban and industrial communities on the park's southern doorstep.

The main reservoirs are to be found clustered around the southern slopes of the central Beacons. Those in the Taf Fawr valley were created between 1892 and 1927 to supply Cardiff. The Taf Fechan reservoirs, dating from 1895 to 1927, were built to

Conifer meets open countryside: the effect of afforestation at the head of the valley south-west of Talybont.

supply the industrial valleys whilst the large Talybont reservoir serves Newport. Swansea receives some of its water from the Cray reservoir in the western park. There will always be those to whom natural beauty and artificially created lakeland are mutually incompatible. Whilst this certainly holds true for some reservoirs, others have, over the years, settled and blended well with the lie of the land, sometimes even enhancing otherwise bleak and barren mountain environments. Few people, for example, can honestly be offended by the attractive Pontsticill reservoir beneath Pen y Fan, especially when viewed from the slipway of the sailing club on its eastern shores on a day when its waters are alive with colourful dinghies and windsurf boards.

Many of the park's reservoirs are encircled by forestry plantations. The arguments against the ubiquitous, conformist conifer are familiar enough not to require repeating here. The alacrity with which the park's landscape has changed through the introduction of Forestry Commission and other commercial conifer plantations is, unquestionably, disturbing – someone brought back to certain parts of the Brecon Beacons today after a fifty-year absence would have difficulty in recognizing the place.

These forests, the first of which were planted in the 1920s, clothe many medium elevations, again especially in the south of the park. Inevitably, there have been conflicts between the National Park Authority and commercial foresters, though we should at least be genuinely thankful for the imaginative recreational facilities – such as waymarked forest walks, picnic sites and so on – created in the last decade or so by a newly image-conscious Forestry Commission.

Caution, not despondency, is the correct concluding note. Water and conifer woodland between them account for no more than nine per cent of the total land area. The Brecon Beacons National Park in the final analysis, is no victim of the worst excesses of the twentieth century. The area's national park status affirms the fact that this part of south Wales still preserves its wilderness and its natural beauty; that this is a countryside in which long-established traditions, a rural culture and way of life continue to prevail. Farming is still the most important element within the local economy; and Brecon, a barometer for the surrounding farmlands, is definitely at its most animated on Tuesdays and Fridays when the country comes to town for the market and livestock sales.

A stroll through the streets of Brecon confirms this sense of the traditional and time-honoured. A most attractive town, its fabric retains many a charming feature. Narrow, tightly packed streets, passageways and a display of fine Georgian façades characterize its busy shopping thoroughfares. Plentiful evidence remains to remind visitors of the town's long history and evolution from walled medieval community. Nothing much has changed here to invalidate the nineteenth-century description of Brecon as a most pleasant town 'possessing architectural remains which connect it with the most important events of past ages, and surrounded by natural objects of the most sublime and beautiful character'. In fact, that nineteenth-century view is more accurate today than it was a few years back, thanks to the opening in 1980 of a much-needed bypass which routes 'through' traffic south of the town.

Llandovery is another town which, in the complimentary sense of the phrase, looks its age, though it is quite different in character to Brecon. The contrast between the two market towns

Brecon, a medieval seat of power and, today, a busy market centre, is full of interesting old nooks and crannies.

illustrates the linguistic and cultural dichotomy which makes it so difficult to arrive at an agreed definition of 'Welshness'. Separated by a mere twenty miles, Brecon and Llandovery stand at opposite sides of a border between English- and Welsh-speaking Wales. English is the language of the streets in Brecon, whilst Welsh, by and large, is the tongue of the farmers and shopkeepers in Llandovery.

In the Beacons, these differences can be seen as a cultural legacy from medieval times. The Anglicizing influences brought in by the Normans were, as pointed out in an earlier chapter, confined to the lowlands in the east of the park. Norman disinclination to settle further west ensured a continuity of Welsh ways, customs and traditions. This is no fanciful theory, for the 1981 Census gives empirical weight to the argument by establishing a strong correlation between the use of the Welsh language and a westward movement through the park. Around Crickhowell, for example, five per cent or less of the population speak Welsh. This rises to ten per cent in Brecon, thirty per cent in Sennybridge and sixty to seventy per cent in that part of the park further west within the county of Dyfed.

4 **Flora and fauna**

First impressions of the Brecon Beacons are those of scale. Big appears to be beautiful to the exclusion of all else. Mountains roll endlessly away beneath huge skies; a seemingly uniform blanket of moorland and rough pasture clothes empty hillsides as far as the eye can see. The Beacons, highland 'pure and simple' (to repeat an earlier description), are not, it seems, a place for the minutiae of life in its many and varied forms. But despite surface appearances to the contrary, the Beacons Park boasts a great variety of plants and wildlife. This variety springs in part from marked local diversities in soil and rocks, together with their distribution, height and aspects. Furthermore, as a breeding ground for wild plants, the Beacons are helped by a temperate climate and reasonable amounts of sunshine.

The pattern that emerges is surprisingly complex. At the one extreme there are the large stretches of mat grass and fescue moor which give the mountains their appearance of consistency; and at the other there are localized pockets which can throw up items of great botanic interest indeed, including examples of flora almost exclusively – and in one case uniquely – confined to the park.

In all, there are around 850 species of flowering plants indigenous to the park. Those which first catch the attention inhabit the Beacons' vast areas of moor and mountainside, tufty uplands and boggy plateaux. From any lofty viewpoint – or better still, from the air – these pallid greeny-brown highlands exhibit an inexorable uniformity of character: a uniformity convincingly fragmented by any map which identifies the different types of vegetation growing here. Such a map assumes the appearance of one of those impossibly complicated jigsaw puzzles as it identifies the various types of moor and heathland – cotton grass, heather, bilberry and so on – which colonize their own individual patches.

Their genesis, in common with that of other flora in the park, was in post-glacial times around 12,000 years ago (all pre-glacial flora was swept away by the ice sheets). Around 6,000 years ago, the Beacons

Bare, exposed moors, green, rounded shoulders of land and a hint of conifer forest . . . quintessential Beacons landscape.

may have been forested up to about 2,000 feet, above which a mountain tundra of alpine grassland probably took over. Later climatic shifts produced modifications, the timber line dropping to around 1,000 feet in some parts as the slopes were invaded by bog – not to mention the Neolithic, Bronze and Iron Age woodchoppers. Climate and man, working in tandem, thus established a basic blueprint for upland vegetation cover that still exists today.

In the lower grounds up to 1,000 feet (with some variations), a pattern of clearance and cultivation was established. Above this 'cultivation' line, on former forested slopes and high ground, rough grassland and heath – a so-called 'grass-heath zone' – gives way to bog as the altitude increases. The grass-heath zone overlies the poor soils directly above the cultivated fields. This zone includes the *ffridd*, the name given to the large, enclosed, rough pastures one step down from the open, mountain, grazing lands. Plants characteristic of this intermediary zone between lowland and true highland include brown bent, sheep's fescue (both particularly dominant), bracken and other ferns.

Higher still is the exposed – and often waterlogged – 'mountain and moorland zone'.

The Romans built a straight-as-a-dye road—now properly surfaced and still in use—across these moors west of Trecastle.

Regular walkers in the upper reaches of the Beacons can be forgiven for comparing these boggy summits to a vast, saturated sponge which, under every step, issues forth copious amounts of water which only the most impervious of footwear can keep out. Although it appears to be a monotonous expanse of bare moor and acidic bog, this highland is covered with a blanket of vegetation that contains many textures.

Sphagnum mosses are a dominant element in the blanket's boggy parts. These mosses – of which there are many different species – are characteristic plants of the park's badly drained high areas. They vary along with the habitat, some growing on the drier hummocks, others on wetter ground and standing water. Certain flowering plants and grasses also flourish in this wet, peaty environment. Common cotton grass, for example, occupies areas of deep peat throughout the park.

Drainage, peat erosion and the extent of grazing are major factors in determining changes in vegetation. The cotton grass moorland is succeeded by four additional peat-based plant habitats – heather moor and upland heath, bilberry moor and upland heath, fescue and mat grass moor, and purple moor grass. The latter creates another tough, wet environment underfoot – in fact, purple moor grass often takes over from sphagnum as the dominant species – beloved of the masochistic soggy-booted breed of walkers. Such stretches occupy poorly drained areas of redistributed peat on the dip slopes in the rainy central Beacons, Fforest Fawr and Black Mountain.

In the western park, high rainfall, this time

accompanied by freer drainage, has led to a covering of sheep's fescue (a plant that likes poor, well-drained, shallow soils) on areas of redistributed peat. This, in turn, gives fescue moorland and, ultimately, mat grass moor (this succession is explained by the tastes of the sheep – fescue is overgrazed by them, resulting in an increase in mat grass, which the sheep dislike). In the drier Black Mountains, the vegetation covering is more characteristic of areas of lower rainfall. Here, heather and bilberry moorlands are commonplace above deep peat, whilst stretches of shallow, redistributed peat are covered with mat grass.

These peaty moorland communities are acidic, and thus limited in their range of flowering plants. Look out, though, amongst the rough, tufty ground for the occasional faint touch of colour brought by heath bedstraw, tormentil and heath milkwort – and, when it really becomes wet and peaty underfoot, various rushes, sedges, the fly-catching sundew, bog asphodel and bogbean.

Grassland, acid moor, heather and heath may well account for the greatest coverage in the park; nevertheless, it is to the more localized corners of landscape that we must look for the greatest botanical interest. Brownstones from the Old Red Sandstone series can be very rich in lime. Where these rocks are exposed and broken up to form craggy, well-watered slopes, the resulting flora can be very interesting indeed.

Pride of place in any hierarchy of the Beacons' wild plants must go to the arctic-alpines. The park is at or near the southernmost British limit for these plants, which are stubborn leftovers from the end of the last Ice Age. They now hold their ground only in the high mountains and shady north- and east-facing scarps in the central Beacons, the Carmarthen Fans and also on occasional limestone crags elsewhere. The most celebrated alpine cliffs are to be found at Craig Cerrig-gleisiad, the dark cwm in the extreme north-eastern corner of Fforest Fawr. The sun rarely touches the dank cliffs here, which soar to around 2,000 feet providing cool gullies and shelter for species such as roseroot and purple saxifrage. These rare plants (alpines as well as arctic-alpines) enjoy special protection, for Craig Cerrig-gleisiad's cliffs are the nucleus of a 156 acre national nature reserve, established in 1958.

Arctic-alpines can also be seen in other upland locations in the park – Craig Cerrig-gleisiad's neighbour, Cwm Du, and the slopes above Llyn y

The purple saxifrage, a rare arctic-alpine plant that grows in high, sheltered places in parts of the park.

Something you will see nowhere else in the world; Ley's whitebeam is unique to the park.

Fan Fach in the Black Mountain are other good locations, for example. Other plants have gradually crept up into the middling-to-high ground, adding to the variety of flora to be found here. Cowslip, primrose, early purple orchid and wood anemone are some of the 'lowland' plants which have successfully taken root amongst the arctic-alpines. Further variety is induced by a switch from lime-rich to acidic soils (a frequent occurrence in the Beacons), preparing the ground for an appearance by some of the aforementioned acid-loving plants such as heathers, sheep's fescue and bilberry.

The southern fringes of the park ring yet more changes. Here, the flora's characteristics and range of species are determined largely by the Carboniferous Limestone rocks. Particularly characteristic of these limestones are the yew and whitebeam trees. The latter, a relative of the mountain ash, brings to the park its other great botanic celebrity, for the Penmoelallt Forest, on the grey rocks north-west of Merthyr Tydfil, is the only place in the world (apart from one other location on the opposite side of the valley) where Ley's whitebeam grows. Penmoelallt's seventeen acres, designated a forest nature reserve in 1961, is a mixed deciduous woodland mainly of ash and oak, a type gradually disappearing in Wales. Its location right next to a flourishing conifer plantation gives its presence an added poignancy.

Ogof Ffynnon-ddu, further west near Craig-y-nos Country Park, is another nature reserve on the limestone belt. In addition to its quite exceptional speleological relevance as one of the largest cave systems in Britain, Ogof Ffynnon-ddu's status as a national nature reserve (established in 1975) also reflects the significance of its flora. Its 1,021 acres, although dominated by heather moorland and acid grassland, also contain small areas of limestone grassland which support interesting plants such as limestone bedstraw and mountain everlasting; and in amongst the crevices of the small sections of limestone pavement grow specialities such as mountain melick, lesser meadow rue and lily of the valley.

Two more national nature reserves, in the eastern Carboniferous outcrop, are Cwm Clydach and Craig y Cilau. The former, established in 1962, is a fifty-five acre site in the deep limestone gorge carved out by the River Clydach. The inaccessibility of the native beechwoods here – one of the few remaining in Wales and also, incidentally, at or near

Craig Cerrig-gleisiad: the sheltered cwm and nature reserve of Craig Cerrig-gleisiad, haunt of the raven and sanctuary for rare arctic-alpines.

Limestone litters the hills in the upper reaches of the Tawe valley north-east of Abercraf.

beechwood's western limit in Europe – probably saved them from the axes of the seventeenth- and eighteenth-century charcoal-burners who decimated the tree cover elsewhere in the gorge. This mature woodland, right next door to industrial south Wales, is regenerating well, as are the mosses and ferns which flourish in its shady glades.

Craig y Cilau, to the north-west of Cwm Clydach, overlooks Llangattock and Crickhowell. Like Ogof Ffynnon-ddu, it is a national nature reserve for reasons both subterranean and above ground. The cave system here is of great scientific interest, as are its rock faces, crags and screes. Established in 1959 over 157 acres, this is the best known of all the botanically significant limestone outcrops in the park, and is mainly notable for the variety of rare or local trees that grow here. In common with Cwm Clydach, its natural beechwoods are close to their western limit. Rare whitebeams (including the very rare lesser whitebeam) also grow here, together with large and small-leaved limes.

Coed y Castell is a local nature reserve in the far west of the park near Carreg Cennen Castle. This thirty-nine acre reserve, established in 1976, is particularly fascinating due to its contrasting habitats. Carboniferous Limestone, with its characteristic ash woodland cover and floristically interesting rock ledges and grasslands, underlies the west of the reserve. In the east, Old Red Sandstone takes over, where the dominant tree is oak and the open lands are covered by bracken.

This is as good a place as any to sound a note of warning concerning the park's nature reserves. In all, there are eight (four national nature reserves, three local nature reserves and the one forest nature reserve). More details on most of these reserves – including specific information on public access – are included in this book's gazetteer section. However, it is worth emphasizing here that whilst some allow free access, the public are asked to keep to established footpaths and rights of way.

Ystradfellte's 'Waterfall Country' is yet another limestone area rich in botanic interest. In its deep, shady ravines and gorges, ferns are particularly prolific (green spleenwort, hart's tongue, brittle bladder and hard and soft shield ferns all grow here under a covering of ash trees).

The limestone gorges – the more remote the better – retain some of the best native broad-leaved woodlands. Today, only scattered relics of the

The River Mellte tumbles through a steep, wooded gorge south of Sgwd Clun-gwyn, the 'White Meadow Fall' in the heart of Ystradfellte's 'Waterfall Country'.

Beacons' former thick forest cover remain, usually in small blocks or along inaccessible slopes (Cwm Clydach is an outstanding example). Oak, birch and alder are among the main species, with beech occurring in some areas. The extent of the decline in natural woodland is put into sharp perspective when we learn that broad-leaved trees today account for considerably less than the nine per cent of the land area in the park taken up by commercial forest.

The cultivated lowlands, for so long tamed by farmers' field systems and the like, are not without their interesting nooks and crannies. Unfortunately, the meadow flowers (yellow rattle, eyebright, whorled caraway and meadow thistle for instance) which, until fairly recently, were so widespread in the fertile farmlands have mostly fallen victim to grassland improvement schemes. Devil's bit scabious, globe flower valerian and various orchids once brightened peaty pastures. Occasional patches of colour in hedgebanks and overlooked corners are signs that at least a few – but only a few – have escaped. Aquatic vegetation displays similar antipathy to the hand of man. Floristically, the reservoirs in the park are of little interest. Most

Unimproved wetlands in the Senni valley, though the land here is nothing like as boggy as it is in the wastes of Fforest Fawr on the southern horizon.

attention focuses on Llangorse Lake, the largest
natural lake in south Wales. Unfortunately, this
valuable habitat – important for its flora and fauna –
is under threat from pollution and heavy
recreational use (a thorny issue which is dealt with
more fully later on in the book). Nevertheless, it still
supports a rich vegetation. It is surrounded by
particularly fine alder and willow groves whilst
waving reed grass, bulrush and the rare fringed
waterlily are amongst the many species to be seen
in its marshy shallows.

The Beacons Park provides its bird life with
habitats ranging from sheltered stretches of inland
waterway to lofty mountain crags. The variety in
species is, correspondingly, a wide one; not only
that, but the populations are quite plentiful,
especially in lowland areas. Over 200 different
kinds of bird have been recorded in the park, of
which about 100 breed here.

Birds, like any other creature, have their
preferred habitats. Some make for the rough, open
high ground, others seek the shelter of wood and
forest. Some rely on the plant and fish life found in
the park's lakes and reservoirs, others hunt the
fields and hedgerows for food. Some less adaptable
birds need specific, well-defined habitats whilst
others compound the permutations – not to mention
confound the ignorant bird-watcher – by surviving
in a variety of conditions. Furthermore, some birds
migrate whilst others of the same species are happy
to remain in their chosen habitat year in, year out.

Experienced ornithologists familiar with the
manifold nuances of bird behaviour will have
unravelled such potentially confusing traits many
times before. For the less experienced bird-
watcher, who might leave his armchair for only
occasional forays into the hills, we can at least deal
in broad categorizations here by linking certain
birds to certain types of habitat.

Birds characteristic of the high moorland, crags
and mountains that cover so much of the park are
the raven, kestrel and buzzard. The black raven,
large of body and loud of croak, is a particularly
frequent sight in the skies above gloomy Craig
Cerrig-gleisiad, the craggy cliffs of which are a
long-established nesting haunt for the bird.
Buzzards are also quite commonplace, circling
above the moorland as they scan the wastes for
small rodents. The kestrel, longer in tail than the
buzzard, hovers for prey above moor and
farmlands. Two highland birds that can only be seen

in spring and summer are the wheatear (easily identified by its white rump) and ring ouzel (otherwise known as the mountain blackbird because of its similarity to the familiar blackbird apart from its white, crescent-shaped bib). Both birds nest amongst rocky terrain and gullies.

Lapwing (or peewit – so named after its distinctive call note) are commonly seen in large flocks in late summer and autumn. Two of the easiest birds to spot on the high grasslands are the skylark and meadow pipit. These small brown birds (the skylark is the larger of the two) are the most numerous breeding birds in the uplands. The peregrine falcon and red kite, on the other hand, are only seen very infrequently – indeed, keen bird-watchers often return home frustrated after long and fruitless vigils.

One of the rarest birds of prey in the park is the peregrine falcon.

The reclusive peregrine falcon, when it does make an appearance, usually nests in the great crags also favoured by ravens and kestrels. The extreme rarity of the red kite gives it an air of prized exclusivity – so much so that it has almost become a point of honour, for those living in or near the park, to have seen it. Within Britain, this bird is confined to the remoter parts of central Wales, though it sometimes ventures into certain parts of the Beacons. My initiation into the select group of kite-spotters was thanks to this book's photographer, Colin Horsman. He lives at an undisclosed (and suitably obscure) spot somewhere in the west of the park with the bird for a neighbour.

Another upland rarity is the red grouse. Not so long ago, grouse were shot here in significant quantities. At the turn of the century, for example,

There are delightful riverside walks beside the Neath between Pontneddfechan and Pont Melin-fach, a few miles to the north.

Park near the crest of the mountain road between Pontsticill and Talybont — known locally as 'the Glyn' — and make the stiff, sharp ascent to Craig y Fan Ddu.

Blaenavon grouse moor yielded between 300 and 400 brace a season. Although they have declined since, a scattering of these birds – remnants of the most southerly indigenous population in Britain – still frequent the heather moor in the south-eastern corner of the park. Heather moorland is also the habitat of the merlin, another of the park's breeding birds.

The Beacons' woodland cover throws up two distinctly different habitats – the deciduous wood and the conifer plantation. The former has the advantage of offering a natural environment, diverse habitats, wide range of foods and nesting sites; so, predictably enough, it attracts the greater variety of species, particularly in the breeding season when the broad-leaved glades are very lively with birds.

The park's oak, birch and ash woods welcome a mixed bunch of summer visitors from Africa. The wood warbler, as its name implies, is a highly audible bird which, despite its yellow throat and breast, can be more easily heard than seen. The redstart is a pretty, small bird, distinguished by its fiery orange-chestnut rump and tail, whilst the pied

flycatcher (the male, with its striking black-and-white plumage, is easily the most conspicuous) is particularly interesting since it tends to be concentrated in the broad-leaved woods of Wales and northern England. The tree pipit is another common broad-leaved species, and many other summer visitors also put in an appearance, including the spotted flycatcher, chiffchaff, blackcap, whitethroat, willow warbler and garden warbler.

All in all, over thirty species breed in the park's deciduous woodland. Not all of them are summer migrants. Of the resident birds, both the tree creeper and nuthatch are numerous. These attractive birds, a pair of accomplished tree climbers, can often be seen making jerky but assured progress up a trunk. Other all-year-round residents include the woodpecker, chaffinch, robin and various tits. Buzzards and sparrowhawks also find the woodlands ideal nesting places from which to hunt, both in the high moors and pastoral farmlands.

Conifer forests, although offering far less in the way of variety, can still be occasionally rewarding to bird-watchers. The versatile tree pipit can again

Old woodland survives in isolated pockets. This narrow band, along the upper reaches of the River Tawe, is surrounded by bald hillside.

The pied flycatcher is attracted to the Brecon Beacons' remaining broad-leaved woodlands.

be seen, along with the whinchat (its favourite perch is on the tops of small conifers), grasshopper warbler (another bird that is heard but not often seen – listen out for its uniform high-pitched trill) and wood pigeon. Few species are attracted to the really thick forests, where close-planted Sitka spruce trees almost merge with one another to block out the light. Two of the exceptions are the small coal tit and the even tinier goldcrest.

The park's farmlands, well endowed with hedgerows and scattered groups of trees, provide sheltered nest-sites – and a convenient source of food – for quite a few species. Magpies, rooks, carrion crows and jackdaws are commonplace, as is the smaller bullfinch, a handsome bird easily picked out by its distinctive pure white rump and rose-pink breast. Other finches and seed-eating smaller birds – the chaffinch, greenfinch, goldfinch and yellowhammer amongst them – can be seen in the hedgerows or foraging in the fields from the late summer onwards.

With so many rivers, streams and lakes in the park, one could be forgiven for anticipating a rich aquatic birdlife. But there are problems. The rivers, although profuse, are fast running and thus poor in the plant life on which the water birds feed; and Llangorse Lake, for so long a safe haven for many species of year-round residents and migrant visitors, is now the subject of a conservation controversy. The natural beauty and ecology of the lake have been upset by its heavy use as a water sports venue and the enrichment of its water with nutrients, possibly derived from agricultural fertilizers. Until 1981, it was also on the receiving end of a substantial local output of sewage effluent.

We know that Llangorse was noted for its bird life even in medieval times, for the twelfth-century chronicler, Giraldus Cambrensis, tells a story in his journals of the birds at Llangorse which sang only for the rightful ruler of Wales. Pollution and disturbance in the last thirty years have had serious effects on the bird and plant life. The number of underwater plants is now very few. Unless present efforts to control and manage the situation are successful, will the birds finally depart?

Llangorse is still, despite the problems, a mecca for ornithologists. The lake's reedy, marshy borders are an ideal place from which to study a wide variety of waterfowl. The great crested grebe, for example, a confirmed fish-eater and expert diver, can be picked out on the waters by its

The Talybont reservoir, winter home for large populations of wildfowl.

distinctive, tufted, double-horned crest and long neck. The black birds with white foreheads are coots, whilst the heron, long of leg, neck and bill, can be seen poised like a grey sentinel in the shallows ready to stab a passing fish. Llangorse's reed beds are also an important habitat, providing a roost for thousands of starlings. Interestingly, the lake is almost on the western limit of distribution for the reed warbler, a summer visitor. The sedge warbler, a commoner relative, also nests around the extensive reed beds as does the reed bunting.

Autumn and winter are the seasons of greatest ornithological activity at Llangorse and the nearby Talybont reservoir (only about four miles away as-the-heron-flies). These are the times of the year when the migrant birds – some very rare – drop in. The birds are discovering that man-made reservoirs have uses other than the supply of water, for some – Talybont in particular, and to a lesser extent those in the Taf Fawr and Taf Fechan valleys – are becoming refuges for bird life. Ironically, peaceful Talybont has helped beleaguered Llangorse maintain its bird populations, since species can easily commute between the two. Indeed, such is the importance of Talybont's wildfowl that the reservoir was made a local nature reserve in 1975. Established by the national park through agreement with the Welsh Water Authority and the Forestry Commission, the reserve covers 490 acres – most of which is water – and is managed by the Brecknock Naturalists' Trust. The fact that access is restricted is no real handicap, since ornithologists have an excellent vantage point from the minor road running along the western shore.

The goosander, a regular winter visitor to certain stretches of water in the park.

Talybont and Llangorse are noted for their duck populations. Species such as the familiar mallard and smaller teal, in addition to the less well-represented pochard (an energetic diving duck) and tufted duck (a black-and-white diver) may be present all year, though it is in the winter season when supplemented by migrants that their numbers are largest. Those that can generally only be seen in winter include the goosander (a large duck with salmon-pink underparts), the goldeneye, the gregarious widgeon and the whooper swan.

The dipper and grey wagtail are two of the few birds happy to congregate along the Beacons' rapid rivers and streams. These two breeding water-birds – their names reflect the characteristic mannerisms each displays – have been known to nest as high as 1,500 feet. Kingfishers also breed widely, particularly along the placid Monmouthshire and Brecon Canal. Other aquatic birds which can also be seen include the moorhen and water rail, both of which frequent ponds and rivers; also the common sandpiper, which nests by still or running water at many altitudes.

In the distant mists of time when the tree cover was thick, man needed to be on his guard against some of the savage beasts that roamed wild here. From remains discovered in limestone caves, we know that bear and wild ox were amongst the mammals, long extinct, that once populated the Beacons' hills and woods. Wolves and red deer were common until their forest habitats were destroyed (though there is evidence that the latter may well have lingered here until as late as the seventeenth century). Today's visitors to the park need not worry unduly about unfriendly wildlife, except for the occasional recalcitrant pony on Llangorse Common who, on being refused his fair share of a picnic lunch, promptly seeks revenge by kicking the car belonging to the parsimonious picnickers (this is not folklore – I have seen it happen). Apart from the street-wise Llangorse breed, there is no threat from the mountain ponies of the park (which are, incidentally, not wild but bred for sale); still less from the docile sheep that populate the slopes in their countless thousands, though motorists should be warned that these sleepy creatures tend to wander haphazardly across the roads and have yet to come to terms with the internal combustion engine.

The largest true wild animals now left in the park are the fox, badger and otter. Foxes and badgers

The Monmouthshire and Brecon Canal is a favourite location with the kingfisher.

A familiar sight in the Beacons — the ponies that wander the open moors and mountains.

are quite numerous. Badger setts are common and the animal is well established here, partly because of its protection under the law. The otter, on the other hand, has not been so fortunate. Once fairly common along many of the park's stretches of water, it has suffered in recent years from the familiar catalogue of environmental problems (water pollution, destruction of river-bank habitats and the like).

The polecat, a smaller relative of the otter, has benefited from an almost opposite experience. This nocturnal hunter is managing very well indeed – especially since it was under threat of extinction early this century (it is, in fact, almost extinct in England). Its survival – and, judging by its increasing numbers, new lease of life – in various parts of the park (and mid- and north Wales) is not unconnected with the freedom from persecution it now enjoys thanks to the decline in game-keeping.

Occasionally, deer are reported, and several recent sightings of muntjac deer suggest that the numbers of this dainty introduced species may be increasing in the park. Stoats and weasels are common, as are rabbits, hares and squirrels (as the immigrant grey has increased by leaps and bounds over the last forty years, the native red squirrel has unfortunately declined to the point of extinction).

Other smaller mammals which are well established in the park are a few species of vole, the wood, house and yellow-necked mouse, mole, hedgehog, common and pygmy shrew. Less widespread, but still represented locally, are the water shrew, harvest mouse and dormouse.

Bats have long been noticed here, flitting amongst

The tenacious polecat survives – and apparently thrives – in various parts of the Brecon Beacons.

the trees and over waters, but as protected species (under the Wildlife & Countryside Act, 1981) they are now being more systematically recorded. Some eight or nine species have been identified, the lesser horseshoe being known to form colonies up to three miles underground in the limestone caves. Neglected tunnels and old buildings also provide the roosts to which large colonies regularly return.

If you are extremely fortunate (or unlucky, depending on your attitude to wildlife), you may come across a snake with dark zig-zagging markings down its back. This is the adder, the only poisonous British reptile. It appears, rest assured, only infrequently in the park, as does the only other snake here, the harmless grass snake. More widespread are the common lizard and slow-worm (which, contrary to popular opinion, is not a snake but a species of lizard).

Of the amphibians, the common toad and common frog are numerous, especially in the lowlands. The smooth newt is also attracted to the lowlands, though the smaller, more widespread palmate newt occurs right up to quite high altitudes. The Beacons' prized fishing rivers need no real introduction. The Wye and Usk have their salmon and brown trout; and the latter fish, along with rainbow trout, also inhabits the park's well-stocked reservoirs. Llangorse Lake (*Llyn Syfaddan* in Welsh) is well known for its pike, roach, bream, perch and carp – and most of all for its very large eels (there is a local expression, 'as long as a Syfaddan eel'). Perch, roach and pike are also frequent in the Wye, roach and pike, together with dace, also favouring the muddy waters of the Monmouthshire and Brecon Canal.

The field vole is one of the three species of vole to be found in the park.

Llangorse Lake suits the dragonfly. The lake's reedy shores and shallows are good locations at which to view a number of species. One representative, the golden-ringed dragonfly, must be a hardy traveller for it has also been spotted at around 2,000 feet in the lonely heights of Craig Cerrig-gleisiad. There are no guarantees concerning the appearance of another species, the *Ischnura pumilio*. This is a very rare dragonfly indeed, its breeding ground in the park being one of perhaps only two in Britain.

Over twenty species of butterfly have been recorded in the Beacons, including the comma (in the south-eastern park), the rare marsh fritillary (seen on boggy ground), the brimstone, grayling and white-letter hairstreak, these last three species not often seen in this part of Britain. The small heath

is the only butterfly which is a common resident on
the high moorlands (though it is often joined by
migrants such as the large white and sometimes the
red admiral and painted lady).

Beetle-lovers will need to devote plenty of time to
the Beacons, for there are hundreds of different
species here. Quite easily the star of the show, on
the strength of its bizarre Antipodean lineage, is the
Cis bilamellatus. This species was imported,
probably inadvertently, from Australia to London
from whence it spread to various parts of England. It
arrived in Wales in 1959 and by 1962 had happily
settled at the Sgwd yr Eira waterfall.

Although it is probably safe to assume that those
readers who have reached this far into the book are
not about to wreak havoc with wildlife by indulging
in an orgy of anti-conservationism, it may be worth
clarifying the main points of the law affecting
species. These can be summarized as follows. It is
illegal to kill, injure, take or sell specially protected
wild animals such as the otter, badger, red squirrel
and all bats (and many non-mammal species); also
to disturb almost all of these animals in their places
of shelter. All wild birds, their nests and eggs are
protected (with exceptions for pest and sporting
species), and there are special penalties for
harming certain rarities. Specially protected plants
must not be uprooted, picked or sold, and
uprooting any wild plant (except on your own land
or with permission) is illegal.

5 The park today

The National Park Authority might disagree, but, for me, there is no more succinct or tangible an expression of the innate conflict between conservation and recreation than the sight that greets travellers as they approach Storey Arms from the south along the A470. A mile or so before Storey Arms, the flat-topped summit of Pen y Fan comes into view, weather permitting. Within another half mile, a straggling, broken line of walkers can usually be picked out against the mountain's muted moorland greenery. Closer still the damage that their boots are causing becomes fully apparent. A red scar – gully-deep in parts where the erosion is at its worst – marks the line of ascent. Efforts are continually being made by the National Park Authority to repair the erosion on this, the most obvious and over-used route to the summit

The popularity — and vulnerability — of the central Beacons is self-evident in this well-trodden footpath, one of the main routes to Pen y Fan.

of south Wales's highest peak.

When I first walked to the top of Pen y Fan in the mid-sixties, I also followed this obvious route, which starts from the roadside at Pont ar Daf. The differences then, compared to today, are difficult to exaggerate; I probably run the risk of inviting incredulity by mentioning them. For a start, the path, green and tufty underfoot, was no more than a sheep track in places; and I shared the mountain with no more than thirty or forty other walkers, even though it was a pleasant early summer Sunday. Today, someone *always* seems to be trudging up that muddy red footpath, whatever the weather or time of year (I drive past Storey Arms quite frequently and have yet to see the mountainside entirely devoid of walkers).

Pen y Fan's problems spotlight the basic tensions facing this area and, to a greater or lesser degree, Britain's other nine national parks. The parks were created in the heady post-war years to preserve and promote; in the words of the National Parks and Access to the Countryside Act of 1949, their role was that of 'preserving and enhancing the natural beauty of the areas' and 'promoting their enjoyment by the public'. These worthy sentiments, uncontentious enough on paper, are often difficult to reconcile in practice, though in fairness to their originators we are speaking with the benefit of hindsight. The inherent contradictions did not begin to come to the surface until the late fifties and sixties through the growth in leisure time, affluence and personal mobility. By the time I came to walk to the top of the Beacons, cars were becoming commonplace at weekends on the quietest of country lanes in the park. The Beacons were busy acquiring a whole new audience, for the park was now within a few hours' drive of millions of people.

By the sixties, the foundations on which our national parks had been built were beginning to creak with these contradictions. The dual aims – conservation on the one hand, public enjoyment on the other – were revealed as being increasingly incompatible. Nothing has changed to make them less so. The challenges that the park now faces are manifold; more so since the seventies, when a third element concerning the 'welfare of the local people' became part of an overall National Park Plan, published in 1977. And the issues do not end there. Changes – and fresh challenges – have come from new farming methods and trends in agriculture, and from the spread of commercial conifer forests.

The area around the Craig y Ddinas rock near Pontneddfechan is rich in both geological interest and industrial heritage.

There have been changes, too, in the role which the Beacons play in supplying populous south Wales with its water.

The National Park Authority can at least now look to helpful guidelines laid down by a government review in the seventies which recommended that, where the needs for conservation and recreation cannot both be met, the former must have priority. Ultimately, the Park Authority is in the unenviable position of trying to balance an unruly equation. Equilibrium is difficult when you have to keep conservation to the forefront and at the same time avoid alienating your millions of visitors. Farmers, rightly preoccupied with making a living, further alter the equation; as do the commercial foresters and the water authorities, all of whom have to be considered along with the walkers, hang-gliders, pony-trekkers and the tourists to whom a good day out in the country involves – quite legitimately – nothing more than a car ride to a suitably scenic lay-by or parking area. Then again, on top of everything else the Park Committee also assumes the responsibility of the local planning authority for the area, routine planning control occupying a good deal of time and effort. The Park Committee, as well as anyone, knows the truth of the old maxim 'You can't keep all of the people happy all of the time'.

A broad awareness of the aims and objectives of the national park is a necessary backcloth against which to view contemporary issues. To understand 'The park today' we need to look at its beginnings, even though the Beacons are now very different from what they were in 1957, the year when they were given national park status. One of the major

Stop off for a picnic on the A470, a few miles north of Storey Arms.

changes can be summed up in a single word: tourism. In Britain's post-industrial twilight, the service and leisure sectors of our economy – according to some economic gurus – represent the only rays of sunshine. Whatever validity that argument might have, no one can dispute the considerable influence that tourism has brought to bear on the Brecon Beacons in the last twenty years.

Tourism is one of those infuriatingly imprecise, elastic words with a multiplicity of meanings. Everyone immediately identifies the tourist as some visitor from away who stays at an hotel, guest house or self-catering cottage for a 'proper' holiday. But the definition can apply much closer to home, though few people recognize it. *I* am classified as a tourist to the park when I jump in the car and drive the six miles or so from my home to Ystradfellte's 'Waterfall Country'. In fact, by so doing I contribute to the largest sector of those seeking recreation in the Beacons – its day visitors.

The park's resident population of 32,000 seems an insignificant figure compared to the millions of visits that are now made annually to the area. Two-thirds of this total is made up of day visits, the remaining one-third accounted for by the more traditional 'tourist' – the holiday-maker staying for a few nights or longer. This well-defined pattern is an interesting one, demonstrating that the Beacons' proximity to large local populations is clearly more influential than the fact that it is also the nearest national park to London and the south-east of England. This is by no means a common pattern; in the Pembrokeshire Coast National Park, for example, the reverse applies with holiday-makers outnumbering day visitors.

The contribution which tourism brings to the local economy is much more difficult to quantify. Again, the more obvious manifestations of the growth in travel and leisure – in terms of hotels, restaurants, attractions and the like – are easy enough to identify. Brecon, for example, has in recent years graduated into a thriving little centre. The town, with a population of 7,200 the largest in the park, is an obvious focal point of tourist attraction and now boasts some excellently refurbished hotels and new eating places. In addition, there now exists a reasonable selection of hotels, country inns, guest house and 'bed and breakfast' accommodation, caravan and campsites, youth hostels and self-catering cottages throughout the park. Visitors are also, increasingly, turning to farmhouse accommodation as more and more farming families supplement their income through tourism. Less obviously, but arguably more crucially, tourist spending is percolating its way through the entire economy, boosting the takings in local shops, garages and pubs. It also helps to create extra jobs by working as an 'invisible generator' of growth within the service and leisure industries, and to

Ice-bound and myth-laden: the waters of Llyn y Fan Fach beneath Bannau Sir Gaer in the Black Mountain.

maintain year-round facilities which the local population alone could not support.

Tourism brings its benefits – and its problems. The downtrodden path to Pen y Fan is a severe case, though in no way representative of the overall situation. I would not want to leave you with the impression that the Beacons are today nose-to-tail with tourists' cars or toe-to-heel with walkers' boots. Apart from a few black spots, the great glories of these mountains – the sense of space they impart, their essential emptiness and wild and windswept natural beauty – still remain uncompromised. I recently walked, once again, up to the shores of remote, icy-black Llyn y Fan Fach then upwards still further on to the razor-sharp crest above to the summit Fan Brycheiniog. I saw hardly a soul; and was reminded of a similar day, over twenty years ago, when I was first introduced to this unchanging mountain fastness (though spirits were, as I recollect, lower on that Sunday as we pondered our collective fate in the fog whilst our formerly omnipotent leader – an over-ambitious teacher – inconclusively tapped his compass with all the authority of the captain of a sinking ship).

It is quite impossible to begin to do justice in these pages to the walking opportunities within the Beacons. Such a subject deserves another book, another time. Suffice it to say that the park is walking country *par excellence*, better suited to this pursuit than many other upland areas in Britain because of the uninterrupted progress which walkers can make for hours on end across consistently high ground, usually above 2,000 feet and beyond any tree cover, without recourse to scrambling or climbing.

This sense of space and open-ness is partially due to the nature of the terrain – that rounded, weathered Old Red Sandstone again making its presence felt. It is also largely a consequence of the vast areas of open or common land in this part of south Wales, covering over forty per cent of the park's 519 square miles. Access to these huge tracts of land is the key to the walker's enjoyment of the Beacons. The freedom to roam over uncultivated mountain and moorland was one of the main aims behind the creation of the park in the first place.

Although, in strictly legal terms, the public has access to only fourteen of that forty per cent, in practice they can walk across almost all of it (though they are sometimes confined to rights of way) as long as farmers' interests are respected. A further

Sharp ridge and swooping escarpment—a typical Beacons combination— at Graig Fan Ddu south-east of Pen y Fan.

factor which keeps the 'Great Outdoors' open to everyone is the guaranteed free access which the public has to the core of the park, thanks to its ownership by the National Trust. This crucial area, the central mass of common land in the Beacons themselves, includes the highest peaks and covers 8,192 acres, two and a half per cent of the total area of the park. The National Park Committee itself also owns or manages some 21,570 acres, about six and a half per cent of the park's area, the majority of which is common land. The lion's share of this came from the purchase, in February 1984, of 21,414 acres – about half in Fforest Fawr, and also including the important Mynydd Illtud Common around the Brecon Beacons Mountain Centre – from the Eagle Star Insurance Company. This acquisition demonstrates the high priority given to the protection not only of landscape but also to the access which the public has enjoyed in practice, if not as of right, for many years.

It comes as no surprise to learn that walking is easily the most popular activity here. There are almost 1,000 miles of paths, as well as many 'green lanes', in the park. Although not legally responsible for them, the recreational use of these paths is

obviously of much interest to the Park Committee.
Park staff carry out some clearing, repair, stile-
building and waymarking; and also negotiate
'permissive' (permitted) paths to overcome local
difficulties for walkers and/or landowners. It is
hoped that, eventually, all public paths will be
brought up to a basically accepted standard. But
with such a high mileage and so little in the way of
resources, a list of 'priority paths' has been
compiled. In addition to this practical path work, the
Park Committee also publishes a variety of walks
booklets and leaflets to help visitors enjoy the area
without causing problems to landowners.

The exhilaration which springs so generously and
freely from walking in the Beacons always needs to
be qualified by a cautious respect for the ever-
present dangers. On a clear day, the green and
undulating Beacons may not look as challenging as
the rugged, rocky pinnacles of, say, Snowdonia. But
make no mistake, this fickle, deceptive terrain is
mountainous in every sense of the word. Conditions
above 1,500 to 2,000 feet can change alarmingly
quickly, catching out even the best prepared
(amongst the many to have fallen victim to the
Beacons' rain, mist, cold and lack of shelter have
been well-equipped soldiers on mountain
exercises).

The most poignant reminder of the park's
dangerous character can be seen on the ridge
north-west of Corn Du above Lyn Cwm Llwch, the
small lake in the central Beacons. A monument here
marks the spot where the body of five-year-old
Tommy Jones was found. In August 1900, Tommy
and his father were on their way from Brecon to visit
relatives in a farm in the valley. Meeting some of the
family on the way, young Tommy ran ahead with a
thirteen-year-old cousin. The cousin returned alone
and, despite repeated efforts to find him, poor
Tommy perished high on the mountainside.

Although serious walkers eschew – and often
denigrate – them, the waymarked footpaths
established by the Forestry Commission have their
part to play. Such walks are particularly popular
with family groups looking for a less demanding
day out in the country than one spent in the moors
and mountains. Whatever the stout-booted brigade
might say or think, such walks at least divert visitors
away from some of the busier, more popular parts
of the park into quieter corners which can accept
them with equanimity.

In this respect, the Forestry Commission is to be

applauded for the initiatives it has taken since the early 1970s. Woodlands that were once uninviting are now open to the public. Many forests now have their car parks, picnic sites, walks, interpretive facilities and – in the case of Garwnant in Coed Taf Fawr along the shores of the Llwyn-on reservoir north of Merthyr Tydfil – a Forest Visitor Centre complete with children's adventure playground.

The walks through the woods largely avoid paths through tediously regimented rows of conifers. At Garwnant, for example, there are pleasant walks along the mountain stream from which the centre takes its name; and at the head of the Talybont Forest there is a most attractive short walk – another favourite of mine – through the trees and past abandoned farmsteads to the Blaen-y-glyn waterfall. Whilst I am once again revealing personal preferences I will also mention a few *bona fide* mountain walks which come high on my list: the ascent of Pen y Fan from the 'Gap' route – a possible Roman road – north of the Neuadd reservoirs (much, much better than the standard, over-walked drag up from Storey Arms); sections of the authentic Roman road of Sarn Helen across lonely Fforest Fawr; the Grwyne Fawr trackway as it climbs into the Black Mountains east of Talgarth; sections of the long-distance Offa's Dyke path along the park's eastern boundary; and, of course, almost anywhere in Ystradfellte's 'Waterfall Country'.

So many different activities now take place in the park that it is tempting to look upon the area as one huge outdoor pursuits centre, catering for all predilections. Pony-trekking is very popular, a 1984 survey revealing that about 900 ponies were in use at trekking centres throughout the park. Everyone from complete beginners to experts can feel at home, especially in the Black Mountains where there is a particularly good choice of centres. As with walking, the appeal of this pastime in the Beacons derives largely from the access which riders enjoy to the high ground, though in this case the sturdy little Welsh cobs and ponies do most of the work.

Other pursuits and pastimes include angling, caving, some rock-climbing (often in abandoned limestone quarries), water sports, canal cruising – even hang-gliding and dry slope skiing. It is fair to say that, whilst there are some contentious issues – the Pen y Fan footpath, power-boating on Llangorse Lake, and some bridlepath erosion caused by the hooves of too many ponies are leading candidates

Better than any ice sculpture. The Blaen-y-glyn waterfall (accessible by path from the road between Pontsticill and Talybont), almost shrouded in a complex canopy of ice.

amongst them – most of these outdoor activities do not dilute or compromise the fundamentally peaceful, unspoilt landscapes at the very heart of the national park's *raison d'être*.

Activities are often combined with education at many of the outdoor centres which have sprung up. Youngsters in schools and colleges from many parts of Britain come here on courses, possibly combining a little canoeing or caving with field studies into conservation issues, geology, land use or archaeology. The park staff themselves are heavily involved in assisting educational groups – and providing information and facilities for the public. The prime site in this respect is the Brecon Beacons Mountain Centre, near Libanus, which attracts around 150,000 visitors a year. Opened in the mid-sixties, it soon proved popular with car-borne visitors as well as walkers. The wide audience the centre attracts enjoy wonderful clear-day views of Pen y Fan and its neighbouring peaks from a vantage point on the shoulder of Mynydd Illtud Common. Outdoors, pleasant walks (some of them with guides) can be taken across the common whilst indoors the centre (open all year except Christmas Day) serves as a source of information and advice on all aspects of the park. Conservation and a respect for the countryside are, quite obviously, implicit themes here, though it is refreshing to see that they are communicated to a popular audience in a way that is never dogmatic or stridently counterproductive. The centre's relaxed ambience seems to impart a caring attitude to the environment all on its own; and, quite apart from anything else, they make an excellent cup of coffee in the downstairs buffet area.

The popular Brecon Beacons Mountain Centre, near Libanus, attracts a wide range of visitors — everyone from weary walkers to families enjoying a day out in the country.

Craig-y-nos Country Park is also a delightful place to visit. Set in a steep-sided valley carved by the River Tawe, this forty acre park was once the ornamental grounds fashioned to accompany the even more ornamental Craig-y-nos Castle. This rambling nineteenth-century sham, still standing above the park, was the home of Madame Adelina Patti, the internationally famous opera singer. Her 'pleasure grounds' – a most attractive area of river meadows, fields, wood and lakelands – have, since 1976, been open to the public under the management of the National Park Committee. Craig-y-nos, incidentally, is almost next door to the Dan-yr-Ogof showcaves complex, the most popular tourist attraction in the park. This proximity is mutually beneficial, for the neighbouring sites offer between them a full day out for visitors –including a growing number of educational groups – to this part of the Beacons.

The public can look not only to the Mountain Centre for advice, but also to three Information Centres (open seasonally) at Brecon and the two 'gateway' towns of Abergavenny and Llandovery. For those more seriously interested in the Beacons, there is the Park's Danywenallt Study Centre.

For some of the best views in the Beacons, take a walk along Mynydd Illtud Common from the national park's popular Mountain Centre.

Ornamental grounds match the ornate mansion at Craig-y-nos Country Park, near Abercraf.

Tucked away in the Talybont valley, this centre was converted from a traditional farm building to provide residential accommodation for up to twenty-five people. Opened in 1977, it offers short courses on a wide variety of subjects ranging from ornithology to rural crafts, and serves as a base for many educational groups studying aspects of the park.

The Park Committee also provides many other services and facilities, such as picnic sites, car parks, an imaginative guided walks programme (something here for everyone) and a warden service. Each warden has to cover a lot of ground – about 130 square miles. The nature of the job is also wide ranging: the warden's multifarious role reflects that of the park itself. Wardens are involved, for example, in both conservation and recreation work. Some of their time is also spent in telling people (residents and visitors) about the park, its countryside, wildlife and so on. The aim, always, is to improve understanding between visitors and landowners, and respect for the park's fabric, while helping visitors to enjoy their stay. Full-time wardens are assisted in their many tasks by part-time paid wardens (working summer

Sheep queuing for winter feed near the frozen Neuadd reservoirs.

weekends), voluntary wardens and many other volunteer groups.

Tourism, as I have said, is a rather woolly term, the extent, basic nature and precise benefits of which are difficult to pin down. No such speculations surround farming, categorically the most significant activity in the Beacons as measured by the amount of land it occupies. No less than eighty-five per cent of the park's total area is designated agricultural land in some form or another (enclosed holdings accounting for fifty per cent, common land grazings the remaining thirty-five per cent). The great majority of this land is devoted to upland and hill farming – specifically, the rearing of hill sheep and beef cattle. The small amounts of arable farming that do take place are mainly subservient to pastoral demands, involving crop growing for animal feed (hay and silage making, swede and barley growing). Dairy farming is of relatively minor importance.

Livestock farming takes place on altitudes high and low. On the hill and upland farms, sheep and beef cattle are reared for sale as breeding stock or for fattening on lowland farms. There are around

850,000 sheep in the park. Many of these hardy animals spend much of the year away from the enclosed lands around the farm itself out on the open rough pastures higher up – hence the importance of these common lands on which farmers have the right to graze stock. The flocks are only brought down for lambing (late March and

The transition from lowland field systems to open mountainside can be easily seen in the Tarell valley just north of Storey Arms.

April) and shearing (late June or early July); also sometimes to lowland farms or on 'tack' to other areas in the winter months. The only real variation in this pattern is found in the more sheltered main river valleys, where less hardy breeds of sheep are reared.

Some farms also own Welsh ponies, bred for trekking and riding. These resilient beasts also spend most of their year out on the high open common, their presence near the roadsides at lower altitudes a sure sign of severe weather. Very few of the park's 80,000 cattle, on the other hand, are found on high ground. Their home is the rough pasture or improved grassland within the farmer's enclosed fields. This enclosed farmland also includes the crops grown for animal feeds, of which grass is by far the most important. Farmers rely on the summer harvesting of grass to provide the bulk of winter fodder, either in dried form as hay or as silage, made from moist grass. Of the other crops grown, swedes are the most common.

These farming customs and practices, though long established, are not immune to change. The 'big is better' theories inherent in the economies of scale have not only found favour on the factory production line. Agriculture escalates to 'agribusiness' as smaller farms amalgamate into larger holdings. National trends such as these, however, have not been directly mirrored in the Beacons, where the hillsides and valleys remain far less affected than in many parts of the country (about two-thirds of the farms here are still owner-occupied). There has been a small decline in the number of farm holdings here (from 1,202 in 1974 to 1,125 in 1981) accompanied by a correspondingly modest increase in the number of larger farms. More significant – and worrying in conservation terms – is the decline in rough grazing (as a proportion of all agricultural land it fell from twenty-seven per cent in 1974 to eighteen per cent in 1981) as it becomes improved to give better quality grass and arable land.

Changes in traditional farming practices, whatever their extent, have implications all the way down the line, from the 'grand design' of the Beacons' landscape to the flora and fauna dependent on the old farmland habitats. The pressures for higher output have meant that land has to carry more stock, with the result that old herb-rich meadows have very often given way to improved pastures of the ubiquitous rye grass. Bigger holdings are part of a general movement towards larger, more easily managed fields. These extended fields imply the destruction of previously familiar features such as hedgerows and walls, a decline hastened by the reduction in the agricultural labour force (about 1,800 people are now employed in full-time farming here, eleven per cent of the park's workforce). Old meadows are lost through drainage and improvement, valuable wildlife habitats destroyed by fertilizers, weedkillers and so on.

Farm buildings also bring their conservation problems. On many farms, the traditional stone buildings, pleasing to the eye and harmonious in their setting though they may be, are increasingly outliving their usefulness. New, larger structures in modern materials are replacing them though they can – and often do – blend in with the background if suitably designed and sited. The park has at least some voice in all of this. Larger farm buildings require planning permission, and since 1980, the Park Authority has been notified of all grant-aided farm improvements so that any conservation implications may be considered. Many schemes are cleared without objection and the number of formal objections are very few indeed; but there is often a

A medieval barn—one of the few surviving outbuildings—at Llanthony Priory.

conservation benefit when a modification is negotiated – for example, park staff can point out that with little or no agricultural sacrifice, a scheme can be amended to retain an existing feature or create a new one. Such 'existing features', perhaps regarded by farmers as 'waste' ground, may be important to wildlife or significant in landscape terms. Sometimes, awkward areas of land can be developed for conservation. Moreover, the operation of this farm grant system helps improve mutual understanding between farmers and park staff.

In practice, for most of the time there is relatively little conflict between the interests of the farmer and the Park Committee. The inevitability of change is accepted. Farmers, like any other businessmen, are guided by commercial and practical motives; and the park, after all, is a living, working environment that is evolving all the time. One of the National Park Committee's own documents sums the situation up well by recalling that the Beacons' first farmers, Neolithic man, initiated the process of tree felling – a destructive one if judged by today's conservationist tenets – which eventually gave this area its

gloriously open hill country, a feature highly prized
and possessively guarded today. Not even the
Brecon Beacons, it seems, can escape history's little
ironies.

Late summer haymaking
in the farmlands south-
east of Trecastle.

From what has already been written, it is apparent
that the Park Committee's powers are not as wide
ranging as is often supposed. As with farming, the
normal activities of the forester are not subject to
planning controls – despite the dramatic change in
the landscape which new plantations may introduce.

About nine per cent – around 30,000 acres – of the
park's area is covered by commercial forests
(double the amount of natural broad-leaved and
mixed woodland cover); commercial forests really
began to make an impact in the inter-war years.
Many were planted in the 1930s, and also in the
1950s and 1960s, largely along the southern dipslopes of the Beacons. These fast-growing forests,
concentrated in large plantations such as Coed y
Rhaiadr (in the Neath valley), Taf Fechan, Taf Fawr
and Talybont, have now reached maturity and
dominate their hillsides. Along with others – mainly
at Glasfynydd (near Trecastle), around the Usk
reservoir and in extensive areas of the Black
Mountains – they constitute the main factor in

landscape change in the park in the last fifty years or so.

Fresh planting has taken place in more recent years across some 1,980 acres in the Fforest Fawr area and elsewhere. A voluntary panel convened by the Park Committee considers proposals for such afforestation, and is often able to agree whether or not they are acceptable. In the end, however, the key decision on the payment of forestry grants may not reflect the Park Committee's view, which is firmly opposed to any further planting of moor and heathland. Something of a test case was lost in 1986 when the Secretary of State for Wales gave final grant approval for yet another small dark patch within the moorland landscape. In these circumstances, the Committee continues to press for the afforestation of bare land to be brought within planning control, with the opportunities for consulting the public that this would provide.

The aesthetic objections to conifer forests are probably engraved on every conservationist's heart. No matter how laudable the initiatives taken by the Forestry Commission, its detractors will always be offended by those serried ranks of evergreens that march unswervingly across the landscape often at odds with the irregular and complex shapes and contours of the terrain, creating a badly matched blanket for its bed of moor and mountainside. One conifer, the Sitka spruce, is particularly commonplace. Foreigner that it is, this species would seem to be tailor-made for the Beacons since it thrives in wet, cool climates and at relatively high altitudes.

In addition to the radical effects these forests have on the look of the landscape, they can sometimes play havoc with wildlife habitats. But it would be unfair to the commercial forester to conclude on an entirely negative note. The Forestry Commission has demonstrated a long-established concern for wildlife, conservation and the provision of recreational amenities. We have to accept that the forests are there, first and foremost, to produce a return on capital. This overriding preoccupation places a severe limitation on measures that might be described as being more altruistic and environmentally beneficial, though the Commission has shown that it is not unsympathetic to public opinion and has encouraged certain changes. For example, the old razor-sharp, straight-as-a-dye edges to the forest, which merely accentuate their intrusiveness, are not repeated in new schemes,

Pockets of surviving deciduous woodland and a patchwork of fields: the view eastwards from Carreg Cennen's limestone outcrop.

where more acceptable, irregular or broken edges related to the contours, are likely to be followed. Broad-leaved trees are generally retained; and the Commission makes grants available to encourage the care and continued survival of such trees outside its own woodlands.

Whilst conifers have marched onwards, there has been a retreat in native broad-leaved woodlands. The area covered by such woods – oak, birch, ash, alder and others – is now extremely modest: only about 12,500 acres, mainly in small blocks. Recorded losses have been considerable since the 1940s (studies in the Black Mountains, for instance, indicate that broad-leaved woodland here may have halved since 1949), though in recent years they appear to have been more limited, offset to some extent by new planting. Heavy stock grazing of old unfenced woodlands, which interferes with natural regeneration, is a particular problem. The spread of Dutch elm disease has also had its effect.

In the face of this decline, the Park Committee has launched an urgent programme of broad-leaved management and restoration to encourage proper care of existing woodlands as well as new planting schemes. Park staff themselves also carry out major tree-planting programmes each winter and further help comes from the Forestry Commission which now gives more generous grants for the rehabilitation of existing broad-leaved woodland and the planting of new trees, together with a set of guidelines for their management.

More often than not, conifer forests ring the reservoirs within the park. There are eighteen in all, most of which – in common with the conifers –

are to be found along the southern belt of the Beacons. The Talybont reservoir, about two miles long and covering 323 acres is the largest, and the tiny Cairn Mound near Brynmawr the smallest. The reservoirs were all created before the park was designated and today supplement their primary function of water supply by making an important contribution to wildlife resources (Talybont's role as a habitat for migrating birds is a classic example) and recreation (most of the reservoirs offer fishing and many now have attractive lakeside car parks and picnic areas). Neither should their scenic contribution be dismissed. Whilst some of them will never be able to mask their alien, man-made origins, others have, over the years, successfully settled into the landscape. In my own view, I would go as far as to say that reservoirs such as Pontsticill, Pentwyn and Talybont now enhance their surroundings. Whatever one's attitude is, it is fair to conclude that, with eighteen in the park, enough is enough. The Park Committee is therefore opposed in principle to further reservoir construction here.

Mineral extraction, mentioned earlier in the book, represents a relatively minor intrusion. There are five active limestone quarries in the south of the park or on its boundary, and one silica quarry worked intermittently. Coal reserves also exist along the southern edge, and several large areas are under investigation by British Coal. Other economic activities, again on a fairly minor scale in terms of their environmental impact, take place at small industrial estates such as the one at Brecon.

As already mentioned, the Park Committee assumes the responsibility of the local planning

They don't often make them like this today. A fine example of the disappearing skills of the drystone-wall builder.

authority for the area. The conservation of traditional buildings and features represents one of its main planning concerns, spurred on by the worrying rate at which historical features – significant architecture, historic buildings, even stone walls – are being lost. The threats come from many sources – from changing land use, highway works, new building development or unsympathetic alterations, and simple neglect and decay.

The park's role as a local planning authority gives it the power to protect historically valuable buildings and features by influencing development proposals and, in the final analysis, by refusing or modifying applications which damage such structures. Sites, features or locations which have statutory designations (listed buildings, conservation areas, ancient monuments and the like) enjoy the inherent advantage of more protection in the planning process. Real powers therefore exist to safeguard our architectural heritage, though hard economic facts often make total preservation difficult to achieve or justify.

In this, as with all the work of the park, resources are scarce. Pressures on the Brecon Beacons – and

Bare hills and trees near remote Llanddeusant in the far west of the park.

all of our national parks – can only increase. If the kind of countryside now synonymous with the Brecon Beacons is to survive, then more effective protection, better management and increased funding are needed. The call for more public spending is always invidious to some; but the plain fact remains that the Brecon Beacons, in comparison with the other parks (some of which face fewer demands), has been seriously under-funded for many years.

In addition to the plea for more equitable financial resources, in 1986 the Park Committee called for legal and administrative changes to help it carry out its statutory duties more effectively. The Committee had in mind, in particular, the following key areas: public right of access to all common land; greater account of conservation needs in the agricultural grant system; planning control on afforestation of bare land; and responsibility for public paths and local plans to be delegated to the Park Committee by county councils.

The Brecon Beacons may still look powerful, indomitable and everlasting, in need of no one's care and protection. But appearances can be deceptive. In this modern day and age, they are more vulnerable than they look.

Selected places of interest

The following gazetteer lists towns, villages, natural features, historic sites, amenities and attractions throughout (and in some cases, just outside) the park. Locations are given by six-figure Ordnance Survey map references (four figures in the case of larger towns). Ordnance Survey maps include instructions in the use of these references.

ABERGAVENNY (SO 2914) An eastern 'gateway' town to the park, just outside its boundary. Stands in the pastoral Vale of Usk close to many attractions. Good base from which to explore Black Mountains and – in immediate vicinity – the 1,955 ft (596 m) Sugar Loaf and 1,595 ft (486 m) Skirrid Fawr. Busy market town (livestock sales every Tuesday and Friday) with excellent selection of shops. Ruined twelfth-century castle in gardens overlooking peaceful fields and the Usk. Interesting, well-presented local museum. Monmouthshire and Brecon Canal nearby. National Park Information Centre, open seasonally, in Monk Street.

BETHLEHEM (SN 683252) Tiny hamlet, more famous for its name – taken from its chapel – than anything else. First-day covers and special Christmas mail franked 'Bethlehem, Llandeilo' are issued from here. Nearby is Garn Goch Iron Age hillfort (see separate entry).

BLAENAVON (SO 2508) Typical old industrial community just south of park. Untypically, both its coal mine and iron-works are now open to visitors (seasonally): there are underground tours of Big Pit and access to the town's historic iron-working complex.

BRECON (SO 0428) Largest town in the park (population 7,200) and obvious focal point. At the confluence of the Usk and Honddu (reflected in its Welsh name, *Aberhonddu*, 'Mouth of the River Honddu'). Long-established settlement and centre of communications. Iron Age hillfort of Pen-y-crug overlooks town; Y Gaer Roman fort (see separate entry) located just over two miles to the west; Norman stronghold and walled borough in medieval times. Ruined hilltop castle (now partly an hotel), fine cathedral and Brecknock Museum, noted for its collection of delicately carved Welsh lovespoons (traditional symbols of betrothal); also South Wales Borderers' Museum which contains a unique Zulu War Room, commemorating defence of Rorke's Drift. Celebrated actress Sarah Siddons born here (in 1755) at a town centre inn now renamed in her honour. Also birthplace of Thomas Coke (1747–1814), influential Methodist missionary with American links. Open-air livestock sales and covered market open every Tuesday and Friday. Good craft and bookshops. Pleasant riverside promenade along the Usk. Administrative centre for Welsh Water Authority, the army, local government and national park. National Park Information Centre near middle of town at Watton Mount, open seasonally.

BRECON BEACONS MOUNTAIN CENTRE (SN 977263) The national park's main visitor centre. Information and interpretation on the whole of the park. Located on the edge of Mynydd Illtud Common providing gentle walking with superb views across to Pen y Fan. Signposted off A470 near Libanus. Open all year, except Christmas Day.

BRECON MOUNTAIN RAILWAY (SO 059098) Narrow-gauge railway running from Pant, on northern outskirts of Merthyr Tydfil, for approximately two miles to lakeside terminus at Pontsticill in foothills of Beacons. Open seasonally.

BRONLLYS (SO 144350) Village just outside park. Noteworthy for its well-preserved Norman motte crowned by a single, stone-built, round tower, added later.

CAPEL-Y-FFIN (SO 256316) Remote religious settlement deep in the Black Mountains. Tiny roadside chapel and, on hillside above, the monastery founded by the enigmatic Father Ignatius (1837–1908), later the home of artist Eric Gill.

CARREG CENNEN CASTLE (SN 668190) Spectacularly located medieval fortress on exposed limestone crag near Llandeilo. Dramatic passageway hewn into cliff face. Superb views. One of Wales's most memorable castles. Nearby is the Coed y Castell local nature reserve (access by path – part of a waymarked walk from carpark below castle).

CASTELL DINAS (SO 178302) Part Iron Age hillfort, part medieval stronghold (though much more survives of the former than the latter). Located near A479, almost 1,500 feet up on a dominant hilltop – a naturally strong site. Walk well worth it for the deep, surprisingly extensive ditches and wide views. Must be one of the highest castles in the country.

CERRIG DUON (SN 852207) Ancient stone circle of twenty-two low-standing stones on wild, empty moorland in foothills of Black Mountains. Maen Mawr, a single stone, stands outside circle.

CLYRO (SO 213438) Village near Hay-on-Wye famous as the home (1865–72) of 'priest and diarist' Francis Kilvert.

CRAIG CERRIG-GLEISIAD (SN 962218) National nature reserve in central Beacons of great significance because of its rare arctic-alpine flora (and some bird species). Access from carpark on A470. Please note that reserve is in private ownership and permission to visit areas away from the public rights of way must be obtained from the Nature Conservancy Council in Aberystwyth.

CRAIG Y CILAU (SO 189158) National nature reserve on limestone outcrop near Crickhowell. Noted for the large Agen Allwed cave system and rare trees (including limes and whitebeams). Access on foot is unrestricted though for activities such as specimen collection, research and climbing, please contact the Nature Conservancy Council in Aberystwyth. Agen Allwed is only open to members of recognized caving clubs.

CRAIG Y DDINAS (SN 914080) Thrusting outcrop of rock caused by a large fault. Nearby is another celebrated geological feature, Bwa Maen, the 'stone arch'. Popular climbing spot; also good starting point for walks up River Mellte and to intriguing silica-mine remains nearby.

CRAIG-Y-NOS COUNTRY PARK (SN 841155) Forty acre country park (managed by the National Park Committee) in former grounds of Craig-y-nos Castle, lavish home of Victorian opera singer Madame Adelina Patti. Landscaped grounds, river meadows, woods and lake. Educational groups encouraged.

CRICKHOWELL (SO 218185) Very attractive small town with fine Georgian architecture beside River Usk. Picturesque thirteen-arched stone bridge, ruined castle, historic St Edmund's church, imposing Tudor gatehouse. Town takes its name from nearby *Crug Hywel* ('Howell's Cairn'), the Iron Age hillfort on the 1,481 ft (451 m) summit of Table Mountain.

CWM CLYDACH (SO 218125) National nature reserve in gorge with thick cover of native beechwoods. Access is unrestricted but permit is necessary for research or specimen collection (contact Nature Conservancy Council in Cardiff).

DAN-YR-OGOF SHOWCAVES (SN 840161) Billed as the 'largest showcave complex in western Europe'. Public access to two cave systems with stalactite and stalagmite formations, narrow passageways and impressively large chambers. Also an archaeological 'Bone Cave', Dinosaur Park, dry-ski slope. Most popular tourist attraction in the park. Caves open seasonally.

DEFYNNOG (SN 925277) Village once more important than its now-bigger neighbour, Sennybridge. Defynnog's church – which has an interestingly inscribed font – was the centre of a large parish which included the Senni valley and much of Fforest Fawr.

GARN GOCH (SN 691243) Most impressive Iron Age hillfort – one of the largest in Wales – with massive stone ramparts. On a 700 ft (213 m) ridge above Vale of Tywi.

GARWNANT FOREST VISITOR CENTRE (SO 004132) Attractively sited Forestry Commission centre in Cwm Taf Forest. Display and exhibition material, forest walks, picnic site, children's adventure play area. Centre open seasonally.

GILWERN (SO 249147) Village at the foot of the Clydach gorge. Good centre for the Monmouthshire and Brecon Canal (boat hire, towpath walks etc.).

GOVILON (SO 268139) Next-door neighbour to Gilwern. Another convenient base for the Monmouthshire and Brecon Canal. The 1,833 ft (559 m) Blorenge mountain – a barrier between rural and industrial south Wales – rises up above the village.

GWERNVALE (SO 211192) Remains of excavated Neolithic burial chamber beside A40 near Crickhowell. Nearby is Gwernvale Manor, now an hotel, formerly home of Sir George Everest (1790–1866), the military engineer after whom the mountain is named.

HAY-ON-WYE (SO 230425) A pretty town bursting at the seams with books. On the last count, there were fourteen major bookshops here, justifying the town's title as 'the second-hand book capital of the world'. Ruined castle, attractive period architecture. On northern approach to the scenic Gospel Pass mountain road below Hay Bluff.

HENRHYD FALLS (SN 854119) Waterfall in wooded gorge with an unbroken drop of around ninety feet, the highest in the park. On the Nant Lech stream near Coelbren. Owned by the National Trust.

LLANDDEUSANT (SN 777245) Hamlet in the Black Mountain foothills. Walkers on the way to Llyn y Fan Fach (see separate entry) should stop to visit the little church here which has ancient roots.

LLANDEILO (SN 632225) Handsome, traditional, old town above Vale of Tywi on western approach to park. Notable single-span bridge across river and, on town's outskirts, ruined Dinefwr Castle on its wooded bluff above the Tywi.

LLANDOVERY (SN 7634) George Borrow, nineteenth-century author of

Wild Wales, called Llandovery 'about the pleasantest little town in which I have halted in the course of my wanderings'. Still preserves its traditional air and architecture. Delightful old town square with covered marketplace. Gnarled shell, remnants of medieval castle, overlooks livestock pens where weekly markets are held (first and third Fridays and alternate Tuesdays in the month). National Park Information Centre, open seasonally, on Broad Street.

LLANFIHANGEL CRUCORNEY (SO 326207) Hamlet at the southern entrance to the Vale of Ewyas and Llanthony (see separate entry). Nearby is Llanfihangel Court, a fine gabled house with Tudor and seventeenth-century features (open to the public on some days spring and summer). Nearby is well-known hill and viewpoint of Skirrid Fawr.

LLANFRYNACH (SO 075258) Neat and secluded little village ranged around its churchyard. Takes its name from St Brynach, a fifth-century Irish missionary. North of the village (about one mile) is a fine stone aqueduct carrying the Monmouthshire and Brecon Canal across the Usk.

LLANGATTOCK (SO 211177) Village of narrow streets and pretty cottages on eastern fringe of Mynydd Llangattock. Stands between the Monmouthshire and Brecon Canal and the River Usk, near to the Craig y Cilau nature reserve (see separate entry).

LLANGORSE (SO 135277) Village centred on church with religious connections as far back as the sixth century. Llangorse Lake (Llyn Syfaddan) lies to the south, the largest natural lake in south Wales (over one mile long). Noted for its rich flora and fauna, especially birdlife, though these are under threat. Popular water sports centre. According to legend,

lake covers an ancient city. Small artificial island – 'crannog' – on which lake dwellers once lived can be seen from shore. Fine views across lake to Pen y Fan. Most visitor facilities concentrated on northern shores. On undeveloped southern shore, at Llangasty-Talyllyn, is a church with an interesting nineteenth-century history.

LLANGYNIDR (SO 155194) Growing village in the Vale of Usk, and close to a particularly scenic stretch of the Monmouthshire and Brecon Canal. The very narrow Llangynidr Bridge (*c.* 1600) really looks its age – cars can just about squeeze over it. The limestone heights of Mynydd Llangynidr loom above.

LLANSANTFFRAED (SO 123234) Hamlet – no more than a scattering of homes – on A40 noted for its church. Here is buried the poet Henry Vaughan (1621–95), whose family came from nearby Tretower Court (see separate entry).

LLANTHONY (SO 288278) Remote hamlet deep in Black Mountains. Its famous red-stoned, ruined priory, dating from 1175, occupies the site of a much earlier religious settlement. Unusual little hotel-cum-inn is now built into the evocative ruins. Nineteenth-century poet Walter Savage Landor bought Llanthony but soon became disenchanted, this miscast lord of the manor leaving under a cloud in 1813, never to return. Good stretches of the long-distance Offa's Dyke footpath (see separate entry) run along the hills above.

LLYN Y FAN FACH (SN 804218) Beautiful, truly remote glacial lake now serving as a reservoir. Lies below the swooping escarpment which guards the northern approach to the Black Mountain. Not surprisingly – for this is indeed a haunting spot – myth and legend surround its waters, concerning a

Lady of the Lake and a local farmer (see Myddfai entry). Inaccessible by car, Llyn y Fan Fach can be approached via Llanddeusant. Walkers can ascend the escarpment above the lake and follow the ridge to Fan Brycheiniog (at 2,630 ft/802 m the highest ground in the Black Mountain), thence downwards to the shores of a second, even more isolated lake, Llyn y Fan Fawr.

LLYWEL (SN 870302) Just off the A40. Noted for its old church which contains a cast of the 'Llywel Stone', an inscribed early Christian monument (another cast can be seen in the Brecknock Museum, Brecon; the British Museum has the original). A second, similar stone – the Taricora Stone – also stands here.

MAEN LLIA (SN 924191) Solitary standing stone from Bronze Age in Fforest Fawr moorland. Visible from minor road.

MAEN MADOC (SN 918158) Another single monolith, alongside Sarn Helen Roman road. Probably erected originally as a plain standing stone, it was later inscribed, in Latin, with the message '[The stone] of Dervacus, son of Justus. He lies here'.

MAESYRONEN (SO 177412) Secluded little chapel, one of the earliest in Wales (1696). Looks more like a farm building than place of worship. Religious dissenters would meet here in secret.

MERTHYR TYDFIL (SO 0406) 'Iron and steel capital of the world' during the Industrial Revolution. On southern gateway to park. At Cyfarthfa Castle, imposing early nineteenth-century home of the Crawshay ironmasters, there is an excellent museum. Wide-ranging exhibits include paintings, eastern antiquity and industrial artefacts.

MONMOUTHSHIRE AND BRECON CANAL Completed in 1812, almost disused by the 1930s, and, since 1968, restored by the British Waterways Board with support from the National Park Committee. Originally an industrial artery, today used for recreation (hire boats, canoeing, fishing and walks along the towpath). Runs for over thirty miles through idyllic rural scenery between Brecon and Pontypool.

MYDDFAI (SN 773302) Traditional Welsh village in lanes south of Llandovery. Linked by legend with Llyn y Fan Fach (see separate entry). A maiden arose from the waters of the lake and married a farmer, only to return to the waters with the farmer's herd of cattle after he had struck her, though only in play. Fact and fiction then begin to mingle, for she is said to have left sons with remarkable healing powers. Coincidentally or not, Myddfai was the home of the famous Physicians of Myddfai, celebrated throughout medieval Wales for their cures.

OFFA'S DYKE PATH Long-distance path from north coast of Wales to south following, wherever possible, the eighth-century earthwork border between Wales and England created by King Offa of Mercia. A section of the path runs through remote hill country along eastern boundary of park between Llanfihangel Crucorney and Hay-on-Wye.

OGOF FFYNNON DDU (SN 867155) National nature reserve of international geological importance as it includes one of Britain's largest cave systems; also interesting flora and fauna above ground. Access by public footpath from Penwyllt. Permit required for off-path access (please apply to the Nature Conservancy Council in Aberystwyth; they can also provide details of access to cave system – permits issued to caving club members only).

PARTRISHOW (SO 279224) Isolated medieval church dating back to eleventh century. Many well-preserved features, but especially noted for its magnificent Tudor rood screen, one of the finest in Wales. A beautiful spot.

PENCELLI (SO 093250) Village right on Monmouthshire and Brecon Canal. A short distance south-west is St Meugan's church (Llanfeugan), a medieval place of worship retaining fifteenth-century features.

PENDERYN (SN 947009) Quarrying and farming village in southern ·limestone belt. Convenient starting point for walks to the wateralls on the Hepste and Mellte Rivers.

PONTNEDDFECHAN (SN 901076) Village near the confluence of the Neath, Mellte and Sychryd Rivers. Exceptional choice of walks, taking in scenic, geological and abandoned industrial sites including gunpowder works: riverside walks beside the Neath and Mellte leading to waterfalls; Craig y Ddinas (see separate entry) and disused mines nearby.

PONTYPOOL (SO 2800) Old industrial town just outside far south-eastern corner of park where the Monmouthshire and Brecon Canal now ends. Contains The Valley Inheritance, imaginative exhibition and audio-visual presentation of industrial and social history.

PORTH YR OGOF (SN 928124) The most impressive cave entrance in the national park. Its gaping mouth, beneath steep cliff, swallows up the Mellte. Also known at one time as the White Horse Cave after the calcite streaks, resembling the head of a horse, on the rocks, a short way inside. A favourite with groups of young cavers. Carparking facilities.

SAITH MAEN (SN 833154) Alignment of seven stones pointing in the direction of Cerrig Duon (see separate entry) about four miles away.

SENNYBRIDGE (SN 920286). Market centre (sheep and cattle) which has grown up because of its location on

the nineteenth-century mail-coach road to Llandovery (now the A40). Also the home of a large army camp to serve the nearby military ranges on Mynydd Epynt.

SGWD CLUN-GWYN (SN 924109), SGWD ISAF CLUN-GWYN AND SGWD Y PANNWR Walking south along the River Mellte from Porth yr Ogof (see separate entry), or from the roadside to the south-west, these three spectacular waterfalls are encountered in the above order (they are all within less than a mile of each other).

SGWD YR EIRA (SN 928099) The most famous waterfall of them all, on the River Hepste. A path runs behind the drop of water. Approach it either from Porth yr Ogof, Pontneddfechan or – the quickest access – Penderyn (see separate entries), or from Clun-gwyn.

SGWD GWLADYS (SN 896093) AND SGWD EINION GAM Two waterfalls on the Pyrddin, a tributary of the Neath. Sgwd Gwladys overhangs in a similar fashion to Sgwd yr Eira. Easily accessible by most attractive path from Pontneddfechan (see separate entry). Sgwd Einion Gam, further upstream, is only for the enthusiastic walker – a river crossing and scrambling are necessary. Well worth it, though, for this is possibly the most dramatic fall of all.

STOREY ARMS (SO 983204) Famous landmark on 1,440 ft (439 m) high point of A470 through central Beacons. Named after landowner Story Maskelyne, though was never, as its name implies, an inn ('borrowed' title from licensed premises, no longer standing, at nearby Pont ar Daf where popular path to top of Beacons now leaves road). Was Youth Hostel for many years. Now an outdoor pursuits centre.

TALGARTH (SO 155338) Old town with narrow streets and period architecture, effectively preserving an air of the last century. Howell Harris (see Trefeca entry), who experienced his great religious vision at St Gwendoline's church, is buried here.

TALYBONT (SO 114228) Very pleasant towpath walks from this village along the Monmouthshire and Brecon Canal with popular hostelries to return to. River Usk flows nearby in its broad vale. Danywenallt, the national park's residential study centre, is located nearby.

TALYBONT RESERVOIR (SO 100190) Local nature reserve on one of the park's most attractive reservoirs. Provides fine habitat for birdlife, attracting large winter population of wildfowl easily viewed with binoculars from minor road along western shore. Information point north of dam. Fishermen can obtain permits from reservoir superintendent.

TRECASTLE (SN 882292) The village acquired its name from the beech-shrouded mound at its eastern approach. This high defensive earthwork, dating from the early twelfth century, is the largest motte and bailey in the park. An even earlier military site – Y Pigwn Roman camp – lies on the Roman road across Mynydd Bach Trecastell a few miles to the north-west.

TREFECA (SO 143322) Hamlet noteworthy for its associations with Howell Harris (1714–73), a leading force behind the Methodist Revival in Wales. The community he founded at Trefeca is now a Presbyterian college; small museum dedicated to this fascinating figure is also on site.

TRETOWER (SO 186214) Village beside Tretower Court and Castle, important historic site which combines fortified keep with a stylish house of the later medieval period. Belonged to the influential Vaughans from the fifteenth to eighteenth centuries (see Henry Vaughan under Llansantffraed entry).

VAYNOR (SO 049106) Scattered hamlet north of Merthyr Tydfil. Vaynor church is burial place of ironmaster Robert Thomson Crawshay (d. 1879). His grave is marked by massive sandstone slab inscribed 'God Forgive Me'. Remains of Morlais Castle (with impressive vaulted basement) stand above limestone quarries to the south.

YSTRADFELLTE (SN 930135) Hamlet close to the River Mellte, and closely associated with the 'Waterfall Country' to the south. A tiny place, pared down to the essential elements – church, post office, pub and a few houses.

Y GAER (SO 003297) Roman fort west of Brecon. Displays fine sections of excavated walls, foundations and gateways. Access via Gaer Farm.

Glossary

English place-names are not common in the Brecon Beacons. They are mainly confined to some of the towns (Brecon – *Aberhonddu* in Welsh – is the obvious example). There follows a glossary of some of the words occurring in Welsh place-names. The names of villages and physical features can usually be broken down quite easily into their component parts to reveal most, if not all, of their meaning. Pen Cerrig-calch ('limestone top'), for example, is particularly easy to translate in its entirety. Others are more difficult, as one Welsh word runs into another, or various mutations take place ('p' sometimes mutating to 'b', for instance, or 't' to 'd', 'd' to dd', 'c' to 'g' and so on).

It is impractical to explain the various rules and regulations here. The following glossary should nevertheless help you on your way to understanding place-names – and picking up a lot of information on the local landscape and physical features in the process. Welsh may still be difficult to pronounce properly, but it is by no means as impossible to comprehend as it first seems.

aber – confluence, river mouth
afon – river
allt – hill, slope, wood
arian – silver, money
arosfa – sheepwalk

bach – little, small
ban, pl. *bannau* – peak, crest (beacon)
banc – bank, hill, slope
bedd, pl. *beddau* – grave
bedwen, pl. *bedw* – birch
berllan, see *perllan*
betws – chapel-of-ease, oratory
blaen, pl. *blaenau* – head, end, source
bod – dwelling
bont, see *pont*
braich – arm, ridge
bren, see *pren*
brith – speckled
bro – region, vale
bron – hill-breast, hillside
bryn – hill
bugail, pl. *bugeiliaid* – shepherd
bwlch – pass
bychan, fem. *fechan* – little, lesser

cadair – seat
cadno – fox
cae, pl. *caeau* – field
caer, pl. *caerau* – fort, stronghold
calch – lime
cam – crooked
canol – middle
capel – chapel
carn, pl. *carnau*, *carnedd* – cairn, rock, mountain
carreg, pl. *cerrig* – stone, rock
castell – castle
cau – a hollow
cefn – ridge
celli – grove, copse

celynnen, pl. *celyn* – holly
cemais – river bends
ceunant – ravine, gorge, brook
cil, pl. *ciliau* – corner, retreat
cilfach – corner, nook
clawdd – hedge, ditch, dyke
clog, pl. *clogau* – crag, cliff
clun – meadow, brake
clydach – torrent
coch – red
coed – wood
collen – hazel
comin – common
corlan – sheepfold
corn – horn
cornel – corner
cors – bog
craig, pl. *creigiau* – rock
crib – crest, summit, ridge
croes – cross, crossroads
crug, pl. *crugiau* – knoll, tump, cairn, hillock
cwar – quarry
cwm – valley, cirque
cwrt – court
cylch, pl. *cylchau* – circle
cymer, pl. *cymerau* – meeting of rivers

dan – under, below
dâr, pl. *deri* – oak
darren, see *tarren*
dau, fem. *dwy* – two
ddol, see *dôl*
deg, see *teg*
derwen, pl. *derw* – oak
dinas – fort
diserth – a retreat
disgwylfa – viewpoint
dôl, pl. *dolau, dolydd* – meadow
draw – yonder
dre, dref, see *tre*
du, fem. *ddu* – black
dulas – dark stream
dwfr, dwr – water
dyffryn – valley

eglwys – church
eira – snow
eithin – gorse
eos – nightingale

esgair – long ridge

fach, see *bach*
faen, see *maen*
fan, see *ban*
fawr, see *mawr*
fechan, see *bychan*
felin, see *melin*
ffald, pl. *ffaldau* – fold
ffawydden, pl. *ffawydd* – beech
ffin – boundary
ffordd – way, road
ffos – ditch
ffridd – mountain pasture
ffrwd, pl. *ffryddiau* – stream, torrent
ffynnon, pl. *ffynhonnau* – spring, well
foel, see *moel*
fron, see *bron*
fynydd, see *mynydd*

gadair (gader), see *cadair*
gallt – hillside (usually wooded)
gardd, pl. *gerddi* – garden
gam, see *cam*
garn, garnedd, see *carn*
garth – hill, height, enclosure
garw – rough, coarse
gelli, see *celli*
gilfach, see *cilfach*
glan – river bank, hillock
glas, gleision – green, blue, grey
gleisiad – young salmon
glyn – glen
goch, see *coch*
goetre – woodland dwelling
gors – bog
graig, see *craig*
grib, see *crib*
groes, see *croes*
gwaun, pl. *gweunydd* – moor, mountain pasture
gwernen, pl. *gwern* – alder, alder swamp
gwrach – witch, hag
gwyllt – wild
gwyn, fem. *gwen* – white
gwynt – wind
gwyntog – windy
gwyrlod – meadow

hafod, hafoty – summer dwelling

helygen, pl. *helyg* – willow
hen – old
hendre – winter dwelling, permanent home
heol, hewl – road
hir, pl. *hirion* – long

isaf, isha – lower, lowest

llan – church, enclosure
llannerch – clearing, glade
llech, pl. *llechau* – slab, stone, rock
llethr – slope
llety – small house, shelter
llwch, pl. *llychau* – lake
llwyd – grey, brown
llwyn – grove, bush
llyn – lake
llys – hall, court
llysiau – vegetables, herbs

maen, pl. *meini* – stone
maenol, maenor – chief's house, manor
maerdy – dairy
maes, pl. *meysydd* – field, plain
mawr – great, big
melin – mill
melindre – mill village
melyn – yellow
merthyr – church, burial place
mochyn, pl. *moch* – pig
moel – bare or bald hill
mynach – monk
mynydd, pl. *mynyddoedd* – mountain, moorland

nant, pl. *nentydd* – brook
neuadd – hall
newydd – new

odyn – kiln
oer – cold
ogof – cave
onnen, pl. *onn, ynn* – ash tree

pandy – fulling mill
pant, pl. *pantau* – hollow, valley
parc – park, field
pedwar, fem. *pedair* – four

pen – head, top, end
pennant – head of a glen or valley
pentre – village, homestead
perfedd – middle
perllan – orchard
pistyll – spring, waterfall
plas – hall, mansion
pont – bridge
porth – gateway, entrance
pren – wood, wooden
pwll – pit, pool

rhaeadr, rhaiadr – waterfall
rhedyn – bracken, fern
rhiw – hill, slope, track up a slope, sloping track
rhos, pl. *rhosydd* – moorland
rhyd – ford

sain, saint, san, sant – saint
sarn, pl. *sarnau* – causeway, old road
sticill – stile
sych – dry

tafarn, pl. *tafarnau* – inn
tal – end
tan – end, below
tarren, pl. *tarenni* – rock-face, precipice
teg – fair, fine
tir – land, territory
tirion – sod, turf, country
tomen – mound
ton – grassland, ley
tor – break (of slope)
traeth – strand, beach, shore
trallwng – wet, bottom land
traws – across, transverse, district
tre, tref – hamlet, home, town
tri, fem. *tair* – three
troed – foot
trum, pl. *trumau* – ridge
twrch – boar
twyn – hillock, knoll
ty, pl. *tai* – house
tyddyn – small farm or holding
tyle – hill, ascent, slope
tywarch – turf, peat, clod

uchaf – upper, higher, highest
uchel – high
un – one

waen, *waun*, see *gwaun*
wen, *wyn*, see *gwyn*
wern, see *gwern (gwernen)*
wrach, see *gwrach*

y, *yr*, *'r* – the
ych, pl. *ychen* – ox
yn – in
ynys – island
ysgol – school
ystrad – valley floor

Bibliography

There follows a short selection of books and maps. A few books concentrate exclusively on the Brecon Beacons; the others feature aspects of the area within an overall, wider coverage of their chosen subjects.

Barber, Christopher *Exploring the Brecon Beacons National Park (A Walker's Guide)*, Regional Publications, 1981.
Condry, William *Exploring Wales*, Faber and Faber, 1972.
Haslam, Richard *The Buildings of Wales: Powys*, Penguin/University of Wales Press, 1979.
Houlder, Christopher *Wales: An Archaeological Guide*, Faber and Faber, 1974.
Howell, Peter and Beazley, Elisabeth *Companion Guide to South Wales*, Collins, 1977.

Mason, Edmund J. *Portrait of the Brecon Beacons*, Robert Hale, 1975.
Thomas, Roger *Journey Through Wales*, Hamlyn, 1986.

In addition to the above, the Brecon Beacons National Park publishes various special-interest booklets, leaflets and map guides; also reports, policy documents and a newsletter. There are also the Ordnance Survey 1:25,000 series of Outdoor Leisure Maps numbers 11 (Central), 12 (Western) and 13 (Eastern); in the 1:50,000 series, almost all of the park is covered by sheet numbers 160 and 161. The Wales Tourist Board publishes various guides on holiday accommodation plus special-interest publications.

Useful addresses

Brecon Beacons National Park
7 Glamorgan Street
Brecon
Powys LD3 7DP
(Tel: Brecon (0874) 4437)

Brecon Beacons Mountain Centre
near Libanus
Brecon
Powys LD3 8ER
(Tel: Brecon (0874) 3366)

Brecknock Naturalists' Trust
c/o Chapel House
Llechfaen
Brecon LD3 7SP
(Tel: Llanfrynach (087 486) 688)

Council for National Parks
45 Shelton Street
London WC2 9HJ
(Tel: 01 240 3603)

Countryside Commission
Office for Wales
Ladywell House
Newtown
Powys SY16 1RD
(Tel: Newtown (0686) 26799)

Forestry Commission
Victoria House
Victoria Terrace
Aberystwyth
Dyfed SY23 2DQ
(Tel: Aberystwyth (0970) 612367)

National Trust
King's Head
1 Bridge Street
Llandeilo
Dyfed SA19 6BN
(Tel: Llandeilo (0558) 822 800)

Nature Conservancy Council
Dyfed-Powys Regional Office
Plas Gogerddan
Aberystwyth
Dyfed SY23 3EB
(Tel: Aberystwyth (0970) 828551)

Nature Conservancy Council
South Wales Regional Office
43 The Parade
Roath
Cardiff CF2 3AB
(Tel: Cardiff (0222) 485111)

Wales Tourist Board
PO Box 1
Cardiff CF1 2XN
(Tel: Cardiff (0222) 27281)

Index

Page numbers in *Italics* refer to illustrations.